Palgrave Advances in the Economics of Innovation and Technology

Series Editor
Albert N. Link
University of North Carolina at Greensboro
Greensboro, NC, USA

The focus of this series is on scholarly inquiry into the economic foundations of technologies and the market and social consequences of subsequent innovations. While much has been written about technology and innovation policy, as well as about the macroeconomic impacts of technology on economic growth and development, there remains a gap in our understanding of the processes through which R&D funding leads to successful (and unsuccessful) technologies, how technologies enter the market place, and factors associated with the market success (or lack of success) of new technologies.

This series considers original research into these issues. The scope of such research includes in-depth case studies; cross-sectional and longitudinal empirical investigations using project, firm, industry, public agency, and national data; comparative studies across related technologies; diffusion studies of successful and unsuccessful innovations; and evaluation studies of the economic returns associated with public investments in the development of new technologies.

More information about this series at
http://www.palgrave.com/gp/series/14716

Dwight Steward • Roberto Cavazos

Big Data Analytics in U.S. Courts

Uses, Challenges, and Implications

palgrave
macmillan

Dwight Steward
EmployStats
Austin, TX, USA

Roberto Cavazos
Merrick School of Business
University of Baltimore
Baltimore, MD, USA

ISSN 2662-3862 ISSN 2662-3870 (electronic)
Palgrave Advances in the Economics of Innovation and Technology
ISBN 978-3-030-31779-9 ISBN 978-3-030-31780-5 (eBook)
https://doi.org/10.1007/978-3-030-31780-5

This Palgrave Pivot imprint is published by the registered company Springer Nature Switzerland AG.
The registered company address is: Gewerbestrasse 11, 6330 Cham, Switzerland

Acknowledgments

We would like to thank Carl McClain, M.A., and Matt Rigling, M.A., for their incredible research assistance. We would especially like to thank and acknowledge the contributions that Carl made to the case examples section of this book. We owe a big amount of gratitude for his research and writing in this section of the book.

We would also like to thank the publishers, including Sophia Siegler, at Palgrave for keeping this project moving.

Contents

CHAPTER 1

Data Analytics and Litigation

Abstract This book examines the use of Big Data and statistical analyses in litigation. This is timely as the use and reliance upon Big Data by business and government has exploded. From a public policy and legal perspective, the implications of this are indeed monumental. Using examples, court decisions, and discussions, we draw connections across many different types of litigation. In business disputes, employment cases, consumer class actions, and even personal injury lawsuits, the analysis of enormous amounts of data often provides evidence that would be otherwise unattainable from witnesses testifying to the facts of the case.

Keywords Big Data • Litigation • Data analytics • Complex litigation

This book examines the use of Big Data and statistical analyses in litigation. This is timely as the use and reliance upon Big Data by business and government has exploded. Organizations of all types are increasingly reliant on analytics and Big Data systems for supporting and informing most, if not all, of their functions. Crucially, in a corollary to More's Law which states that the density of transistors on a circuit board will double every two years leading to doubling of computing power, it is likewise true that the volume of data created and used by business and government doubles every 18 months.

D. Steward, R. Cavazos, *Big Data Analytics in U.S. Courts*,
Palgrave Advances in the Economics of Innovation and Technology,
https://doi.org/10.1007/978-3-030-31780-5_1

From a public policy and legal perspective, the implications of this are indeed monumental. In addition, technological innovation in Big Data as well as areas such as Artificial Intelligence, Internet of Things, and Smart Contracts all have significant implications on how organizations function, privacy, security, how transactions are carried out, and myriad other factors with enormous legal implications. Using examples, court decisions, and discussions from a range of lawsuits and courts, we draw connections across many different types of litigation.

What Is Big Data?

> What's 'big' in big data isn't necessarily the size of the databases, it's the big number of data sources we have, as digital sensors and behavior trackers migrate across the world.[1]

Before proceeding with the discussion on Big Data some clarity is required on the terms that are often used interchangeably. Statistics is properly understood as the use of samples to make inferences about populations. A staple of statistical analysis are surveys, sampling, and testing hypothesis. Statistical analysis is widely used in litigation. Data analysis entails analyzing data of a particular set or population. A financial data analyst examines his firm's stocks, an insurance claims analyst examines her company's extensive claims data, a human resources analyst dives into his agencies' personnel data to assess risk of key staff retiring, and so on. Like inferential statistics, data analysis has been extensively used in litigation (audits, patterns, averages, anomalies, etc.).

Big Data is an elaboration of data analysis but it is also different in ways that have significant implications for litigation. It is not necessarily inferential and relies upon computational techniques which examine patterns, trends, and other features of behavior in the data. Big Data examples are credit card transactions, health insurance claims, and online behavior among others. A key difference between data analysis and Big Data analysis can be gleaned by example. Data analysis generates reports on, say, sales by month. Big Data analysis also examines sales but seeks to find patterns for the effect of time of day consumers shop, the weather, location of store, type of credit card, bundle of goods bought, and so on. Big Data

[1] Jenna Dutcher, "What is Big Data," Data Science at Berkeley Blog September 3, 2014, http://datascience.berkeley.edu/what-is-big-data/

analysis is made possible by the decreasing cost of storage space, the use of cloud computing and the recognition that Big Data analytics can confer a competitive advantage or at minimum efficiency enhancing benefits to an organization.[2]

The National Institute of Standards and Technology defines Big Data as follows: Big Data consists of extensive datasets primarily in the characteristics of volume, variety, velocity, and/or variability that require a scalable architecture for efficient storage, manipulation, and analysis. Further, the Big Data paradigm consists of the distribution of data systems across horizontally coupled, independent resources to achieve the scalability needed for the efficient processing of extensive datasets.[3] While seemingly obtuse, this definition of Big Data has implications for organizational behavior, risk, and ultimately litigation. Unlike merely storing large amounts of data and then analyzing, the use of Big Data requires links among disparate systems, reconfiguring, and/or acquiring complex information system architectures and in increasingly common cases reconfiguring an organization's very structure. For example, Big Data is defined by some as "Big data is not all about volume, it is more about combining different data sets and to analyze it in real-time to get insights for your organization. Therefore, the right definition of big data should in fact be: mixed data."[4]

These processes are complex, expensive, and can be risky. The risk inheres in that organization leadership may not fully understand the implications of using or relying on Big Data. Further, Big Data systems may fail to comply with administrative processes and laws governing the use of personal or confidential data. Combining different datasets is fraught with risk and uncertainty. In addition, true Big Data systems require complex infrastructure at times connected to the internet which expose data and systems to hacking and ultimately legal risks.

[2] Statistical analyses in the form of sampling, quality control, scheduling, operations research, consumer surveys have been a staple of business and government since the nineteenth century. However, with the advent of increased and less expensive computation space and the watershed bestselling 2007 book *Competing on Analytics: The New Science of Winning* by Thomas Davenport the use of big data-dependent analytic methods in organizations of all types grew exponentially.

[3] NIST Big Data Interoperability Framework: Volume 1, Definitions. Final Version 1, NIST Big Data Public Working Group Definitions and Taxonomies Subgroup, September 2015.

[4] Jenna Dutcher, "What is Big Data," Data Science at Berkeley Blog September 3, 2014, http://datascience.berkeley.edu/what-is-big-data/

Data and Big Data in Litigation

In an increasing number of legal cases, large collections of electronic data information, or in some instances Big Data, determine which party ultimately prevails. In business disputes, employment cases, consumer class actions, and even personal injury lawsuits, the analysis of enormous amounts of electronic data often provides evidence that would be otherwise unattainable strictly from witnesses testifying to the facts of the case. In some instances, electronic data is the only way to analyze the parties dueling allegations in a lawsuit.

Lawsuits involving employment discrimination are an area where statistics and Big Data have been used extensively. In employment cases, especially ones involving many plaintiffs, the compilation, tabulation, and analysis of Big Data has been relied upon heavily with the rise of electronic computing. In class action employment lawsuits, litigants frequently introduce mountains of data and analysis to support or refute the allegations of gender, race, age, or other type of illegal employment discrimination.

Litigation in instances of employee unpaid overtime and off-the-clock work allegations is an area where statistical and large data analyses are used extensively. In these cases, commonly referred to as wage and hour cases, former or current employees allege that the defendant illegally denied them their legal right to overtime premium pay, the defendant's timekeeping system illegally shaved work time, or the defendant required them to perform work before or after punching in for work or while punched out for a work break. In these types of wage and hour cases it is typical for parties to present evidence based on the collection and analysis of extensive daily time and salary electronic databases. In some instances, where data is not collected by the defendant, the parties may perform sophisticated statistical surveys, based on the electronic information that is available, to provide insights into the allegations in the case.

In response to the complexity of these cases, a number of courts have established special courts to handle complex cases such as the ones involving massive amounts of electronic data. In California, numerous state courts have been set up to handle complex cases where the judge is particularly well versed in the nuances that these types of complex cases involve. A quick review of the court docket of these complex courts shows that a number of these cases are large employment wage in our class actions that involve the analysis and calculations involving these large electronic datasets. Many of the litigants report that the cases flow more efficiently and a number of the issues are adjudicated rapidly. It is often noted that the monetary cost of establishing and maintaining these types of complex courts is relatively expensive.

The Average Wholesale Pricing (AWP) pharmaceutical drug litigation that began in the mid-2000s is also instructive in the use of large electronic databases information as evidence in litigation. Medical billing data typically conforms to the true definition of Big Data with separate systems communicating, exchanging information, and generating new and enormous sets of data. In these cases, individual plaintiff whistleblowers and state's attorneys alleged that pharmaceutical drug companies conspired to overcharge Medicaid programs for their pharmaceutical products. The plaintiffs in these cases alleged that drug companies fraudulently reported prices to drug pricing reporting agencies that were higher than their actual average wholesale prices. Medicaid programs use the average wholesale price calculated by companies reporting prices to determine the reimbursement to pharmacists for the medicines that they provide to patients. Accordingly, as it is alleged, since the reported average wholesale price was inflated, the reimbursement to pharmacists, and others who receive Medicaid payments, will be inflated.

The analysis of the defendant's actions, and liability, and ultimately the calculation of any damages incurred as a result of the defendant's alleged actions requires the analysis of massive amounts of electronic data. Even in small states with relatively small Medicaid programs, the investigation into the plaintiff's allegations and calculation of economic damages requires the analysis of millions and millions of individual pharmaceutical drug pricing records. The adjudication of these lawsuits required courts to rule on a number of complex electronic data issues. These issues involved topics such as the admissibility of the electronic data and which analyses of the data (and complex relationships among databases as well as algorithms and edits) could be presented to a jury.

Medicaid and Medicare billing fraud audits of medical practitioners such as doctors, dentists, and optometrists is another area where Big Data comes into play. The impact of court decisions in these types of cases is generally magnified given that a number of these cases involve relatively small doctors' offices. In these cases, the state or attorneys working for the state use medical billing records to help determine if a medical professional is defrauding the Medicaid or Medicare system. In the analysis of the medical professionals' billing records, the charging party uses fairly advanced statistical routines to select a sample from the total universe of medical bills to further audit and investigate. Based on the sample, the state obtains additional billing documentation for the medical services and products that were provided and contacts patients to obtain additional information concerning the medical professional services provided.

In instances where overbilling or over reimbursement are alleged to have occurred, the state then uses the sample records to determine the amount of overbilling that allegedly occurred in the entire universe of records. In these calculations the state will typically extrapolate their findings from the sample to the universe and come up with what they believe is an appropriate measure of what the medical professional owes the state. In these instances, the amount that is allegedly owed can easily run into millions of dollars based on the methodology of the state agency. In these cases, the courts are typically run by administrative judges who deal with a range of cases not just the nuanced and specific requirements of electronic data and its analysis. However, the decisions, many of which involve the nuances of the electronic data, that the administrative judge makes can have significant ramifications for both liability and damages.

These examples illustrate the fundamental issues that the judicial system faces when dealing with Big Data and scientific evidence. At an operational level, the courts, often through their role as gatekeeper, have to determine if the scientific data and the supporting analyses are reliable enough to even be seen by a jury. This is made difficult by the constantly evolving nature of data and statistical analyses; some of the analyses that were exotic in the past are commonplace and widely accepted today. It is difficult for a court, or even a practitioner in the statistical sciences, to make definitive statements on the many different uses and applications of the methodologies used in data and statistical analyses. In some instances, a court's reasoning, which is generally based on case law and legal precedents, can inherently conflict with its determinations regarding the admissibility of the data and scientific evidence.

As the use of Big Data and the associated analysis processes change and evolve, the increase in benefits and risks associated with changes of this magnitude will continue in the world of complex litigation. Big Data will potentially have a dramatic impact on how law is practiced, how litigation is undertaken, and how courts make decisions. As noted a few years ago:

> Big Data creates a radical shift in how we think about research … [It offers] a profound change at the levels of epistemology and ethics. Big Data reframes key questions about the constitution of knowledge, the processes of research, how we should engage with information, and the nature and the categorization of reality … Big Data stakes out new terrains of objects, methods of knowing, and definitions of social life.[5]

[5] Boyd, D, Crawford, K (2012) Critical questions for big data. Information, Communication and Society 15(5): 662–679.

References

Dutcher, Jenna "What is Big Data," Data Science at Berkeley Blog September 3, 2014, http://datascience.berkeley.edu/what-is-big-data

Boyd, D, Crawford, K (2012) Critical questions for big data. Information, Communication and Society 15(5): 662–679.

United States Department of Commerce National Institute of Standards and Technology, NIST Big Data Interoperability Framework: Volume 1, Definitions. Final Version 1, NIST Big Data Public Working Group Definitions and Taxonomies Subgroup, September 2015.

CHAPTER 2

History of Data Analysis in US Courts

Abstract Although Big Data may be a new concept, courts have a long history of dealing with statistical and numerical evidence. The types of data and the associated analyses have evolved over time as have the legal decisions and precedents surrounding these types of analyses. These earlier, and necessarily simpler, statistical and data analyses lay the foundations of current, and near future, Big Data litigation. Though the foundations are established, the use of Big Data in litigation requires some changes in analytic approaches.

Keywords Frye • Daubert decision • Expert witness admissibility • FRE 702 • Statistical evidence

Although Big Data may be a new concept, courts have a long history of dealing with statistical and numerical evidence. The types of data and the associated analyses have evolved over time as have the legal decisions and precedents surrounding these types of analyses. These earlier, and necessarily simpler, statistical and data analyses lay the foundations of current, and near future, Big Data litigation.

One of the first recorded uses of detailed statistical analysis in the United States is considered to be the Howland case of 1867. In this case attorney Benjamin Pierce attempted to show that a contested signature on a will had been traced from a genuine signature. Using a basic statistical

D. Steward, R. Cavazos, *Big Data Analytics in U.S. Courts*,
Palgrave Advances in the Economics of Innovation and Technology,
https://doi.org/10.1007/978-3-030-31780-5_2

formula, known as the binomial model, he argued by that agreement in all down strokes of a given signature was extremely improbable.[1] Since this early case, statistical analysis and ultimately Big Data and other sophisticated analytic techniques have become essential features of legal action and litigation. After the Howland case, the use of statistics inexorably grew drawing the attention of some of the greatest American legal minds of the nineteenth century. Consider:

> For the rational study of the law the blackletter man may be the man of the present, but the man of the future is the man of statistics and the master of economics. (Oliver Wendell Holmes, Jr. [1897], 10 *Harvard Law Review*)

This quote from the 1897 *Harvard Law Review* article by Oliver Wendell Holmes, a US Supreme Court justice, on the future of law and the practice of law in the 1890s is as prophetic today as it was then. The use of statistics and data in the courtroom in the 1890s was inherently similar to the way it is used now. This is especially true in civil cases involving business and employment matters. For instance, in the 1890s, after the passage of the Sherman Antitrust Act (1890), the number of cases involving allegations of anticompetitive and/or monopolistic behavior increased significantly. Many of these cases relied upon the analysis of numerical, accounting, financial, and statistical information.

In complex cases, then and now, testimony relying on data, statistics, and ultimately economics is crucial. Moreover, the complexity of these cases has increased as it is not uncommon for the different parties to employ different analytical approaches that can result in the same data, yielding two drastically different conclusions The technical expertise required to meaningfully understand and examine evidence in Big Data cases is likewise greater than that in pre-Big Data times. Still, the early efforts in grappling with statistics, data, and economics all inform the approaches and challenges ahead.

In many cases reliant on or driven by data, it is difficult, if not impossible, for a judge or jury to determine guilt or liability based strictly on the testimony of individual witnesses testifying to the disputed facts. For example, in an antitrust case testimony from witnesses such as company

[1] Meier P, Zabell S. Benjamin Peirce and the Howland Will. J Am Stat Assoc. 1980; 75: 497–506.

executives can establish who talked to whom and can potentially shed light on the nature of certain conversations. However, this type of witness testimony cannot provide reliable evidence of an impact related to the alleged anticompetitive actions. So there may be evidence that company executives talked about collusion and even planned to collude, but what impact did their actions have on the market? Did their alleged anticompetitive actions actually increase prices paid by consumers in the market? Was competition actually restricted by their actions? Did the number of competitors in the market actually decrease? Statistics and Big Data provide insights into these potential impacts.

In antitrust cases, tabulations of large datasets can be performed to measure prices and sales before and after the alleged anticompetitive behavior. Similarly, statistics can be constructed to measure the number of competitors in the relevant product market both before and after the alleged illegal acts. Statistics, however, can only go so far and since they are ultimately just numbers and counts of numbers.

As Oliver Wendell Holmes predicted over 100 years ago, this is where economics comes into the picture. The economic analysis and interpretation of the statistics are ultimately what provides the insights into the allegations in these cases. Economic methodology and modeling provides the framework to make sense of the numbers. In the instance of antitrust allegations, statistics in concert with economic analysis allows the court to compare the outcomes of the actual pre- and post-event statistics to what would be expected from a competitive market and non-colluding participants. Statistical and economic testimony in these instances provides evidence on the likelihood that a competitive market, with non-colluding market participants, would naturally arrive at the price and sales level that is alleged to be the result of illegal acts. This type of approach is used to answer a wide range of questions in litigation involving business and employment matters.

Economics, statistics, and data analysis-based testimony is subject to challenge like other types of evidence that are introduced into a legal proceeding. The avenues and approaches that the courts have dealt with using this type of testimony as evidence have evolved since Oliver Wendell Holmes' famous 1897 quote. A very brief history of expert witness testimony involving economics, statistics, and data analysis is discussed in the following paragraphs.

1900–1960s

Between 1900 and 1920, expert witness testimony involving economics, statistics, and data analysis was relatively limited in business and employment litigation. A findlaw.com search of the US Supreme Court cases over this time period shows that there were dozens of cases on the US Supreme Court docket that involved antitrust, anticompetitive behavior, business torts, or employment disputes. In a number of these business and employment cases economic or statistical expert witness testimony was introduced by either one of the parties or both. During this time period, economic and statistical expert witness testimony was most often provided by company or industry representatives and frequently involved industry or firm practices and limited number of actual numerical calculations. Generally, in these early instances of economic and statistical expert testimony there was little to no mention of a challenge of the admissibility or reliability of the underlying evidence.

Courts also made use of a fair number of "special master" appointments during this time period. Special masters were tasked by courts to perform specialized calculations and provide advice on certain, usually technical, issues. Special masters were typically subject matter experts, such as accountants or business executives, that possessed certain specific knowledge that courts relied on to help them understand specific topics.

Overall, there are limited examples of data and economic expert witness testimony being challenged during this time period. The 1920s US case, *SPILLER v. ATCHISON, T. & S. F. RY. CO.* (1920), is one notable example of a case that utilized data and economic expert witness testimony that was discussed by the court. In this case, the court's discussion of the expert witness evidence portends the changes and standards for expert witness testimony that would be set by 1923 with the *Frye v. U.S.*, 293 F. 1013 (D.C. Cir. 1923) ("Frye") decision.

In this case, the plaintiffs alleged that Atchison, Santa Fe Railroad, overcharged for freight deliveries. In the course of the lawsuit, the plaintiffs took their case to the Interstate Commerce Commission (ICC) and presented expert witness testimony on a number of accounting and financial issues that relied on the relatively complex analysis of numerical information. The trial court awarded the plaintiffs economic damages for the overcharged rates.

On appeal, the Circuit Court of Appeals reversed the trial court. The Circuit Court of Appeals severely criticized the evidence of the plaintiffs, characterizing it as hearsay. The plaintiffs primarily relied on the expert witness testimony of a member and leader of one of the organizations, the Cattle Raisers' Association, that was a party in the lawsuit. The court said:

> Mr. Williams, assistant secretary of the Cattle Raisers' Association, who had gathered the data upon which the claims were based, mostly from commission merchants, in some instances from the cattle shippers. He had prepared the claims, had spent much [253 U.S. 117, 130] time and pains in investigating them, and in the course of his duties had visited several of the points of destination and examined the books and records of the commission merchants to ascertain the method in which their business was conducted and records kept. It was he who testified as to the customary course of business of cattle shippers and commission merchants. He had been connected with the Cattle Raisers' Association for about eight years, and might be presumed to have some general familiarity with the business in addition to that gained in the special study he had made of it while investigating the claims. His explanation of the method of business and the details of the claims was accepted, and accepted without objection, very much as the testimony of an expert witness might have been accepted.

The court ultimately agreed that the use of his testimony was acceptable and admissible. What is notable about this case is that the court went through the witness experience, background, and general qualifications in making its determination that the evidence was admissible as evidence. The type of discussion in this case, which is one of the earlier examples of such a discussion, portends the framework for the admissibility of data and other expert evidence that would be provided in future legal cases.

Frye v. United States, 293 F. 1013 (D.C. Cir. 1923) provided the first framework for the admissibility of data and expert testimony. In Frye, the US Supreme Court provided specific guidance on the use and admissibility of expert witness testimony. While the case did not specifically deal with economic, financial, or statistical data, this case established the guidelines for the admissibility of all types of data for decades and is still relevant in various state courts across the United States.

In this case, the defendant, who was convicted of the crime of murder, attempted to introduce the results of a "systolic blood pressure deception test." The test was supposedly able to determine if a person was not being truthful by studying the changes in the person's blood pressure levels. The trial court in the case ruled the test to be inadmissible evidence. The US court affirmed the appeals court decision and also ruled that the test was inadmissible.

The Frye case is important on two fronts. On one front, Frye codified the role of data and scientific expert witness testimony in legal procedures. Frye solidified the idea that expert witness testimony can be useful when dealing with matters that a typical layperson, be it a jury or a judge, would not have the ability to make an independent and informed judgment about. Data analysis is clearly a matter that would be outside of the area of knowledge of a typical layperson.

The court said:

> The rule is that the opinions of experts or skilled witnesses are admissible in evidence in those cases in which the matter of inquiry is such that inexperienced persons are unlikely to prove capable of forming a correct judgment upon it, for the reason that the subject matter so far partakes of a science, art, or trade as to require a previous habit or experience or study in it, in order to acquire a knowledge of it.[2]

On the second front Frye established the framework for courts to consider when dealing with the admissibility of scientific expert evidence. In essence, Frye required that expert witness testimony be grounded in scientific principles that have gained "general acceptance in the particular field in which it belongs." Specifically, the court said:

> Just when a scientific principle or discovery crosses the line between the experimental and demonstrable stages is difficult to define. Somewhere in this twilight zone the evidential force of the principle must be recognized, and while courts will go a long way in admitting expert testimony deduced from a well-recognized scientific principle or discovery, the thing from which the deduction is made must be sufficiently established to have gained general acceptance in the particular field in which it belongs.

Although the definition of "general acceptance" was subject to much interpretation by different courts, the Frye admissibility was the standard for economic, financial, and statistical expert evidence almost exclusively until the early 1970s.[3]

[2] *Frye v. United States*, 293 F. 1013 (D.C. Cir. 1923).

[3] In the Frye case, the court said: We think the systolic blood pressure deception test has not yet gained such standing and scientific recognition among physiological and psychologi-

1960–1970s

The 1960s saw the rise of modern computing, mainframes, and set the stage for use of Big Data in US courts. During this time period, many of routine business functions and record keeping functions were becoming automated and electronically stored on as electronic data and in electronic databases. Information such as historical product pricing data and employee wages was beginning to be made available in partial if not completely electronic formats. Business and employment data could now be used in conjunction with computer power to crunch basic statistics and tabulations somewhat easily.

Accordingly, the value of electronic data to answer important old questions and to provide new insights into old questions became clear to litigants during this time period. US federal government agencies such as the US Department of Labor (DOL) and Department of Justice (DOJ) as well as private litigants both began introducing evidence based on electronic data at a higher rate during this time period.

Federal regulations and rules, which had begun to directly address electronic data issues, also had an impact on the use of data and statistics during this time period. For instance, the DOL 1961 CFR update provided guidance on employer's time clock system operation and the accuracy of the employee timekeeping data maintained by employers. These 1961 CFR are significant because they demonstrate the DOL recognition of the role of these types of data. The 1961 CFR updates which discussed somewhat small issues, such as how much employee time clock rounding would be acceptable, would provide the basis for how employers maintained data for decades. The accurate recording of employee time has been a focus of DOL investigations since the DOL's early days. By the 1960s mechanical punch time clocks were the standard method of recording an employee's work time.

In 1972, the Federal Court enacted the Federal Rules of Evidence (FRE) that provided a uniform set of rules that would cover all types of evidence, including expert witness testimony involving data and statistical analyses in civil litigation The purpose of the 1972 rules was to "administer every proceeding fairly, eliminate unjustifiable expense and delay, and promote the development of evidence law, to the end of ascertaining the

cal authorities as would justify the courts in admitting expert testimony deduced from the discovery, development, and experiments thus far made.

truth and securing a just determination." Article VII of the Federal Rules of Evidence provided general rules regarding the testimony of expert witnesses and disclosure of facts or data underlying an expert opinion. The 1975 version of Federal Rule of Evidence (FRE) 702 stated that:

> If scientific, technical, or other specialized knowledge will assist the trier of fact to understand the evidence or to determine a fact in issue, a witness qualified as an expert by knowledge, skill, experience, training, or education, may testify thereto in the form of an opinion or otherwise.

While FRE 702 provided courts with a uniform manner for courts to determine when expert witness testimony was admissible in a case, it did not provide guidance on what constitutes reliable expert witness testimony. FRE 702 provided no additional guidance on the "general acceptance" criteria put forth in Frye (1923). In practice, in the absence of additional guidance, a number of courts continued to rely on Frye to determine if the testimony was allowable.

In addition to FREs and Consolidated Federal Regulations (CFR), case law also began to shape how data and statistical analysis would be used in civil cases in the 1970s. In employment and business litigation, there were a number of cases decided by appeals and the Supreme Court that would ultimately influence how data and statistical analyses would be conducted for years. In a number of areas, case law and court decisions arguably had a greater impact than FRE 702 or Frye (1923) on the use of data and statistical analyses in civil litigation.

Castaneda v. Partita, 430 U.S. 482 (1977) and Hazelwood School *Dist. v. United States*, 433 U.S. 299 (1977) are examples of this impact. In this case, Rodrigo Partita was indicted in March 1972 by the grand jury of the 92d District Court of Hidalgo County, a border county in South Texas, for the crime of burglary of a private residence at night with intent to rape. After a trial, Mr. Partita was convicted and sentenced to eight years in prison. Mr. Partita ultimately filed a petition in the Federal District Court, alleging a denial of due process and equal protection under the Fourteenth Amendment, because of gross underrepresentation of Mexican-Americans on the county grand jury.

Statistical evidence supporting Mr. Partita's allegations was introduced at trial. The statistical evidence showed that while Hidalgo County comprised approximately 79.1% Mexican-American citizens, the average grand jury over an 11-year period (1962–1972) was composed of approximately

39.0% Mexican-American citizens. The state did not challenge the reliability or admissibility of Partita's statistical evidence at trial.

The US Supreme Court, upholding the Court of Appeals decision, ruled that the respondent's statistical evidence, and other relevant testimony regarding the grand jury selection process, was sufficient evidence to demonstrate a prima facie case of discrimination in grand jury selection.[4] The court said:

> Given that 79.1% of the population is Mexican-American, the expected number of Mexican-Americans among the 870 persons summoned to serve as grand jurors over the 11-year period is approximately 688. The observed number is 339. Of course, in any given drawing, some fluctuation from the expected number is predicted. The important point, however, is that the [binomial] statistical model shows that the results of a random drawing are likely to fall in the vicinity of the expected value.
>
> The measure of the predicted fluctuations from the expected value is the standard deviation … Thus, in this case, the standard deviation is approximately 12. As a general rule for such large samples, if the difference between the expected value and the observed number is greater than *two or three* standard deviations [emphasis added], then the hypothesis that the jury drawing was random would be suspect to a social scientist.
>
> The 11-year data here reflect a difference between the expected and observed number of Mexican-Americans of approximately 29 standard deviations. A detailed calculation reveals that the likelihood that such a substantial departure from the expected value would occur by chance is less than [1 in a 10,000 billion]. The data for the 2 1/2-year period during which the State District Judge supervised the selection process similarly support the inference that the exclusion of Mexican-Americans did not occur by chance.[5]

The court's analysis is important on a number of levels. On one level, the Court's detailed discussion of standard deviations essentially set a bar for determining if a data analysis and statistical tabulations are to be viewed as statistically significant, or a function of sheer random chance, in the eyes of the courts. As seen above, the court viewed a difference of greater than two or three standard deviations between the expected value and the observed number as statistically significant. In other words, a difference that is greater than three standard deviations is one where the court sees it

[4] *Castaneda v. Partida*, 430 U.S. 482 (1977).

[5] Not by chance: a result not attributable to chance but rather attributable to some specific cause. This is the key concept in statistical significance.

unlikely to have been generated by chance. While the bar that the court set in Castaneda is not always consistent with social science thinking, the "two to three" standard deviation concept has become ingrained in statistical analyses in employment cases.

Second, at a deeper level, the court, by weighing in with the detailed discussion, also provided default guidance on which underlying statistical methodologies could be viewed as reliable in a court setting. The standard deviation approach that is discussed in the Castaneda ruling is specific to certain statistical methodologies, known as classical methodologies, and would not be relevant to other statistical methodologies. The court actually mentioned one classical statistical model, the binomial statistical model, in its decision. Other types of hypothesis testing methodologies that formulate a given statistical analysis statement in a different manner would not lend themselves to the same types of interpretation as presented in *Castaneda v. Partita*. Classical-based statistical methods, such as those relying on the binomial statistical model mentioned in the Castaneda ruling, are the standard and most utilized methods in employment litigation statistical analyses to date.

1980s and 1990s

The 1980s and early 1990s saw even more development of computing power in the business world. Spreadsheets, such as the well-known Excel, and electronic databases, such as Microsoft's Access, were developed and began to be widely used. Personnel information at many employers was routinely stored in electronic databases at this point. Mainframes, as well as personal computers, become more powerful and able to store more data. From the research standpoint a number of the calculations that would have required the equivalent of a supercomputer became possible to do on a desktop.

In the 1990s, the courts became much more of a gatekeeper of data and scientific evidence than at any other point in time. In 1993, the Supreme Court decided on *Daubert v. Merrell Dow Pharmaceuticals, Inc.*, in which the court provided a more rigorous standard of admissibility for scientific evidence. The Daubert decision requires federal courts to apply certain criteria to determine if scientific evidence is admissible or not. These criteria include determining the reliability and known error rate of the analysis and the degree of acceptability of the methodology within the scientific community. The Daubert decision has resulted in stringent guidelines for the admissibility of Big Data statistical evidence that often require the court to make a ruling on the admissibility of scientific evidence prior to trial.

Since the seminal 1993 Daubert Supreme Court decision, federal and state courts across the United States have taken on a role as gatekeeper of scientific, statistical, and ultimately Big Data evidence. However, the case law concerning the use and admissibility of data-based evidence is currently unsettled and evolving. Further, techniques and uses of Big Data are changing rapidly and outpacing case law, posing further challenges and uncertainty. In some areas of the law prior case decisions provide additional guidance on relatively arcane and specific statistical topics while other areas of the law have no substantial case precedents to provide even general guidelines on routine Big Data and statistical concepts.

In any event, Daubert and data-based court evidence often requires judges and juries to become sophisticated consumers of complex statistical information in a short period of time. Judges are frequently required to make critical, case altering decisions concerning complex, and often conflicting, data and statistical analysis methodologies. Similarly, juries are often tasked with weighing the correctness and validity of complicated, competing analyses. The court's role as gatekeeper will be discussed in a later chapter.

References

Castaneda v. Partida, 430 U.S. 482 (1977).

Frye v. United States, 293 F. 1013 (D.C. Cir. 1923).

Holmes, Oliver W Jr, Harvard Law Review 10 (1897).

Meier P, Zabell S. Benjamin Peirce and the Howland Will. J Am Stat Assoc. 1980; 75: 497–506.

CHAPTER 3

Examples of Litigation Involving Big Data Analytics

Abstract The use of Big Data has become common in organizations of all types. Advances in information technology, lower costs of storage of massive amounts of data coupled with increasing sophistication of business processes, and complex compliance and administrative requirements compel modern organizations to store, manage, and rely upon massive stores of data in their daily operations. Industries such as healthcare, securities, and banking use large troves of data and information. These industries have seen a number of notable recent lawsuits involving the use of Big Data analytics. This chapter provides a discussion of several notable cases involving these industries.

Keywords False Claims Act (FCA) • *Qui tam* • Securities and Exchange Act of 1934 • 10b-5 • Fair Housing Act of 1968 • Advertising fraud

Not surprisingly, the use of Big Data has become common in organizations of all types. Advances in information technology, lower costs of storage of massive amounts of data coupled with increasing sophistication of business processes, and complex compliance and administrative requirements compel modern organizations to store, manage, and rely upon massive stores of data in their daily operations. Some industries such as healthcare, securities, and banking are particularly conducive to the use of large troves

D. Steward, R. Cavazos, *Big Data Analytics in U.S. Courts*,
Palgrave Advances in the Economics of Innovation and Technology,
https://doi.org/10.1007/978-3-030-31780-5_3

of electronic data and information. Businesses in these industries have also been involved in a number of notable recent lawsuits that have involved the use of Big Data analytics. This chapter provides a discussion of several notable cases involving these industries.

Healthcare and False Claims Act (FCA) and Fraud Litigation

The healthcare industry comprises upwards of 17% of the US economy. The presence of factors such as those related to third-party payers, insurance, and copious amounts of regulations in a sector where enormous amounts of data, privacy concerns, and allegations of fraud and abuse all combine to generate a significant amount of data-driven litigation.[1] A significant amount of litigation in the healthcare industry is related to allegations of over-reimbursement to hospitals and medical practitioners that provide services to Medicaid and Medicare patients. In the United States, complexity is one of the principal reasons why in 2014 it is estimated that Medicaid made $17 billion in improper and/or fraudulent payments. The analysis of these types of over-reimbursement claims typically involves the assembly of massive sets of medical records and patient billing data and can involve some fairly complex calculations.

A number of these claims are pursued by states and private parties under the False Claims Act (FCA). The FCA imposes liability on persons, contractors, and companies who defrauded governmental programs. The FCA created a civil cause of action against anyone who knowingly presents false or fraudulent claims for payment from the US government. The FCA's *qui tam* provision authorizes private individuals, acting as "relators" (otherwise known as "whistleblowers"), to file a false claim suit on behalf of the government.

According to the Department of Justice (DOJ), the government has collected over $59 billion from FCA suits between 1987 and 2018. In 2018, the US government collected $2.8 billion in False Claims Act

[1] The Centers for Medicare and Medicaid Services (CMS) estimates that in 2017 US healthcare spending reached $3.5 trillion or $10,700.00 per person, this comprising 17.9% of the nation's gross domestic product (GDP). See https://www.cms.gov/research-statistics-data-and-systems/statistics-trends-and-reports/nationalhealthexpenddata/nationalhealthaccountshistorical.html

(FCA) settlements, of which the majority were in the healthcare sector.[2] Of the $59 billion recovered in fraud and false claims cases, over $42 billion (71%) were from *qui tam* or "whistleblower" suits. Of the $42 billion, $7 billion was paid out to relators.

Until the 1990s, a majority of the litigation arising under the False Claims Act were procurement fraud cases against defense contractors. Cases alleging healthcare fraud allegations, however, have increased as spending on Medicare and Medicaid increased. The rise in healthcare fraud cases have involved pharmaceutical companies, medical device manufacturers, hospitals, and doctors. As of 2018, healthcare fraud represented over two-thirds, or roughly $39 billion, of all false claims awards.

Healthcare fraud cases lend themselves to Big Data analyses, as various schemes involve a wide variety of elaborate and complex schemes to improperly bill Medicare/Medicaid. The alleged schemes include selling allegedly faulty equipment, inflating patient's risk assessments, giving kickbacks to providers who recommend certain drugs, upcoding medical services, performing deliberately unnecessary tests, and creating fake patients. As healthcare fraud becomes ever more complex, fact finders are increasingly reliant on large data sources, such as insurance claims, prescription data, and patient records, to determine both the accuracy and scope of fraud complaints under the FCA.

Traditionally, healthcare audits in these types of investigations would require a review of individual claims to determine if provider charges were likely fraudulent. Now, analytical methods, statistical analysis, and Machine Learning algorithms can more easily flag potentially suspicious claims over thousands or hundreds of thousands of records.

Legal cases typically turn on descriptive statistics that describe what has already happened. Thus, the question for a court utilizing data is one of evidence: can the parties prove that a specific fraudulent activity actually occurred at a given time? From the perspective of a Big Data analysis, it is a matter of determining how, and if, the available data supports or refutes the party's claims.

For example, suppose a healthcare provider is accused of submitting inflated reimbursement claims to Medicare. The parties could support their case or refute the claims of the opposing side by examining the provider's billing and patient statistics. In theory, inflated reimbursement

[2] See https://www.justice.gov/opa/pr/justice-department-recovers-over-28-billion-false-claims-act-cases-fiscal-year-2018

claims should be correlated with "abnormally" high provider statistics of some. An analysis may indicate that a given health provider sees far more patients per day than other "similarly situated" doctors. Another analysis could reveal that specific hospitals attract more long distance patients than a similarly situated hospital. A third analysis could show that certain drugs are prescribed at higher rates for specific types of illnesses, or a given test is administered at a far higher rate for different categories of patients. In theory, these kinds of practices will correlate with the provider operating at a higher cost than its competitors, and thus submitting larger bills to Medicare and Medicaid.

If a provider's data significantly deviates from expected norms, it could be argued that this deviation is consistent with the provider's submission of fraudulent claims. If the opposite is true, that is, if the deviation is not sufficiently large, then it could be argued that the deviation is not consistent with the submission of fraudulent claims.

Of course, just because the provider's records deviate from the expected number does not in itself prove the provider committed fraud. For example, it could be argued that the analysis failed to control for other relevant factors, such as patient demographics, the severity of a given diagnosis, the type of hospital, admissions rates for illnesses, or the competency of surgeons performing the procedure. Furthermore, the outcome could be challenged, arguing that the provider filed more claims for the given procedure because the provider's network specialized in the field. Due to the availability of Medicare and Medicaid spending data, structured data sources can be obtained from providers and government sources; such government sources, crucially, allow robust healthcare provider comparisons. Thus, healthcare fraud litigation under the False Claims Act is already primed to pair a Big Data analysis with supporting testimony and documents.

United States v. Community Health Systems, Inc.

A prime example of this type of analysis is *United States v. Community Health Systems, Inc.* In this series of *qui tam* suits filed against Community Health Systems (CHS) in 2011, the plaintiffs alleged that the CHS "embarked on a scheme to increase inpatient admissions from its ERs," disregarding the medical needs of patients, in order to secure higher reimbursements from Medicare. The case, which rested on an analysis of CHS hospital admissions, resulted in a settlement agreement in 2014 where

CHS paid out $98 million to the DOJ and the private relators. At the time, Community Health Systems was the largest False Claims Act settlement in the Middle District of Tennessee, and included other cases filed in Illinois, Indiana, North Carolina, and Texas.

Background

Community Health Systems (CHS) was a healthcare holding company whose affiliated organizations owned, operated, or leased 130 hospitals in 29 states. A separate company, Community Health Systems Professional Services Corporation, managed CHS's subsidiary hospitals and affiliates. Between 2007 and 2010, CHS acquired 59 new hospitals, hospitals mostly in non-urban markets. The plaintiffs alleged that these significant capital commitments led the company to amass large debts, which left the company "significantly leveraged."

The plaintiffs alleged that CHS searched for "nontraditional ways" to increase its profits, including "[deciding] to offer beds to patients who did not meet the criteria for medical necessity," which would increase profits. The plaintiffs contended that the CHS increased its revenues by deliberately admitting patients who did not need inpatient care. At the time, reimbursement rates for a patient receiving inpatient care were $4500–$7000 higher than reimbursements for outpatient care. For Medicare patients complaining of chest pain, their reimbursement rates were "almost $7,000 higher for inpatient admissions than for outpatient observation." CHS received approximately 27.2% of its net operating revenue from Medicare reimbursement claims, or $3.4 billion.

The government and the relators, a licensed doctor and two nurses, relied on interviews of hospital employees and internal documents. When the US government intervened and offered an amended complaint, it noted that a "proprietary statistical analysis originally developed by the Service Employees International Union" and offered by the relators identified 74 CHS hospitals where inpatient admissions "so far exceed [end] national norms" in aggregate and for specific soft diagnoses.

This analysis had to answer two important questions in order to prove relevant to the case. Could the relators' analysis prove CHS hospitals had higher than normal inpatient Emergency Room (ER) admissions? More importantly, could the relators' analysis prove a direct link between ER admissions and CHS practices?

Data

How did the relators'[3] analysts approach these questions in their analysis? First, the prospective analysis required a comprehensive dataset. In this instance, the analysts used Medicare inpatient and outpatient necessary data publically available through the Centers for Medicare and Medicaid Services (CMS). From the two files available, the analysts identified claims which originated from an ER using procedural and revenue codes within the datasets. In order to make an applicable and rigorous comparison of similar claims, the analysts filtered the Medicare data by a series of parameters to insure that the relevant claims were being captured in the analysis. With the dataset assembled, the analysts constructed a number of metrics to compare hospitals and providers and to determine if the data was consistent with the alleged fraudulent activity.

The relators' analysts wished to answer three questions. (1) Did CHS-owned hospitals admit more patients than the national average? (2) Did CHS hospitals admit more patients than the national average for "soft diagnoses" such as non-specific chest pain? (3) Finally, did CHS hospitals admit more patients for one-night stays than the national average?

The analysts thus constructed an "expected ER admissions" rate, which was a metric of how many hospital admissions a given provider should have, which could be compared to the hospital's actual admissions records in the Medicare billing data. This expected admissions rate used the national average ER admissions rate, and then calculated a "normal rate" for each hospital after adjusting for factors like patient age, sex, diagnosis, and the hospital's geographic location (urban or rural).

Using these figures, the analysts compared this expected ER admissions rate with the actual ER admissions rate to come up with a "percent above expected ER admissions." A hospital with a large difference between its actual admissions and expected admissions, therefore, will be an outlier compared to the national average.

Findings

The relators found that the vast majority of CHS hospitals had ER admissions totals which were in excess of national expectations, and their deviations from the national averages were among the highest in the country.

[3] Relator is the term used for a whistleblower in a False Claims Act Case.

The analysis found that most CHS hospitals' ER admissions were far above their expected rates and the national average. In this analysis, the relators utilized guidelines from Medicare to define what was defined as a large outlier. The short-term acute care Program for Evaluating Payment Patterns Electronic Report (PEPPER), designed to help hospitals comply with Medicare guidelines, recommends that hospitals at or above the 80th percentile in admissions (i.e. any hospital with ER admissions higher than 80% of similar hospitals) should receive close scrutiny. According to PEPPER, such deviations are associated with fraudulent claims.

Using PEPPER's guidelines, in 2009, 48 of CHS' 113 relevant hospitals would be considered outliers or about 42.5% of CHS's network. Of 65 hospitals CHS owned for more than three years, 39, or 60%, were at or above the 80th percentile of admissions. Eighty CHS hospitals had ER above their expected rates, given the national average. This came out to 13,714 excess Medicare ER admissions in 2009, representing as much as $68.57 million in overpayments to CHS hospitals by Medicare in 2009. Moreover, 101 CHS hospitals had admissions totals above their expected amounts for non-specific chest pain; of the 101 CHS hospitals, 74, or 73%, were also above the 80th percentile in admissions nationally for non-specific chest pain. So in short, the analysis indicated that CHS hospitals had much higher than expected admissions, given the national average, in 2009.

The analysis up to this point did not link a hospital's ownership by CHS to increased deviations. Indeed, the defense could simply argue that the higher than expected admissions rates at CHS hospitals are a statistical fluke, dependent on factors which the analysis did not capture.

The analysis further looked at the timing of the ER admissions to determine if the rates changed after the hospital was acquired by CHS. Across all diagnostic groups, the average hospital before it was acquired by CHS actually had lower than expected ER admissions rates. The rate was almost 4% lower than the national average. After being acquired by CHS, the same hospital saw its ER admissions rates spike. By the third year of CHS ownership, that same hospital, on average, had an ER admissions rate now 10% above the national average. The data repeatedly told the same story: after a given hospital was acquired by CHS, it saw a continuous increase in ER admissions, holding all else equal.

The relators' analysts confirmed these findings by also examining the expected number of one-day ER stays. Before a given hospital was acquired by CHS, on average its reported one-day visits from the ER were 10% below expected. After just three years of ownership by CHS, the same hospital saw their one-day ER stays spike, on average, 50% above expectations.

Lessons

On August 4, 2014, the relators, the Department of Justice, and Community Health Systems agreed to settle the case. CHS agreed to pay $97,257,500 to the US government and the whistleblowers. In return, CHS denied culpability in the allegations and was released from all other civil or criminal penalties arising under the claims, and all false claims cases against CHS were dismissed with prejudice. The settlement agreement was appealed in 2015, over an unrelated issue concerning attorney's fees.

Cases like *United States v. Community Health Services* are valuable starting points for demonstrating the utility of data analytics in litigation. Data published through government sources are invaluable tools, particularly for false claims cases since public data are generally regarded as unbiased, comprehensive, and neutral. If such data demonstrate a pattern of fraudulent behavior, it carries an extra aura of credibility than a similarly situated private source. Private data sources are no less convincing, and the litigation need not be confined to healthcare for data analytics to be useful.

A recent (and at the time of this book, ongoing) case demonstrating the use of privately obtained data is *United States ex. rel Customs Fraud Investigations LLC v. Victaulic Co*, a *qui tam* case. Victaulic is a global manufacturer and supplier of pipe fittings. The relator in this case, Customs Fraud Investigations (CFI), alleged that for a decade (2003–2013) Victaulic imported metal pipe fitting components from abroad without properly listing the country of origin. By not properly marking its pipes, CFI asserts, Victaulic evaded customs duties that would have otherwise been levied on its imports.

To support its allegations, CFI conducted a two-stage analysis. In the first stage, CFI obtained access to the manifest data of ships importing goods to the United States, a data source maintained by the US Customs and Border Protection Agency (CBP). A third party, Zepol, operated a subscription-based service which allows subscribers to search the manifest data for specific imports or companies. Information slices retrieved from data sources like Zepol, CFI contended, "are considered confidential and treated as such by government agencies."

Through this subscription, CFI searched for all Victaulic imports between 2003 and 2013; in their search, Victaulic acted as a consignee, which meant many of their imports were from foreign subsidiaries. In this time period, CFI concluded that Victaulic imported over 83 million pounds of tubing from abroad (particularly from China and Poland).

Using its own pricing estimates, CFI concluded this represented between 54% and 91% of all Victaulic sales in the United States between 2003 and 2013, or at least $152 million in sales.

After estimating Victaulic's foreign imports, CFI then conducted an analysis of the "secondary market" of Victaulic's products in the United States, in order to determine if these products were properly labeled. To obtain an estimate, CFI conducted a search on eBay, the online auction house and e-commerce site, for sales of "new" iron and steel pipes sold by Victaulic between August 2012 and February 2013. The pipe listings, according to CFI, represented a wide section of US industries, regions, and company sizes. The search results were limited to those sales of Victaulic pipes with images of the product, which were the primary basis for identifying branded pipes and country-of-origin markers. CFI identified 221 unique eBay sales listings for "new" iron and steel Victaulic pipe fittings.

Of those, 29 pipe fittings, 13%, were marked as being made in the United States, while 189 pipe fittings listed, 86%, did have any country-of-origin markings. Only three, or 1%, showed any foreign country-of-origin markings. Upon physical examination of these products, CFI concluded at least 75% of Victaulic pipes were unmarked.

CFI's expert statistician testified that the secondary market for Victaulic products, primarily from eBay, was representative of the United States. The statistical expert concluded, "With 99% certainty," that the percentage of foreign-marked Victaulic pipe fittings was widely disproportionate to Victaulic's actual imports. Backed by witness testimony, CFI asserted that the only conclusion was that Victaulic engaged in a scheme of evading import duties on its pipe fittings.

However, the District Court doubted CFI's statistical methods, and dismissed CFI's claim. In its judgment, the court ruled that the data and statistical evidence CFI presented did not meet the pleading requirements for the Federal Rules of Civil Procedure, 8(a) and 9(b). CFI then appealed the dismissal. In a divided ruling, the 3rd Circuit Court of Appeals reversed the District Court's judgment and remanded the case for further proceedings.

Though the majority allowed the CFI's case to continue, the majority cautioned that it too "was skeptical" of CFI's methods. "There is little evidence to show that CFI's unusual procedure of reviewing eBay listings is an accurate proxy of Victaulic's products available in the United States," the court explained. The majority accepted that CFI established the plausibility of its case, but the majority left one question open: is CFI's evidence convincing.

The dissent needed no prompting to answer this question, arguing that CFI's case consisted "almost entirely of non-random observations" taken off of eBay: constituting little more than "unsupported assumptions and numerical guesswork." The dissent rigorously deconstructed CFI's analysis, beginning with the fundamentals of survey design and unbiased statistical samples. The "eBay Investigation," the dissent argues, is where CFI's claims "ultimately fail." The dissent claims that CFI simply assumes that the products sold on eBay are representative of all Victaulic sales in the United States. Even if this argument was correct, the dissent argued CFI constructed "a subsample of a subsample of a subsample" of the data on eBay. Outlining CFI's entire chain of assumptions, the dissent argued that CFI's chain of inferences "do not support a plausible allegation of fraud."

The dissent said that "CFI gives [the court] ten years of import data and insists there is evidence of fraud [here], somewhere." Yet the plaintiffs are only able to demonstrate fraud "on the basis of statistical evidence alone." *Community Health Systems* is a good lens to examine *Victaulic Co* and the limits of Big Data analyses in fraud cases. Fact finders have to be aware of not only the data on hand, but also the data's relevance to a case. Just because one party has constructed a complex Big Data analysis does not itself lend that analysis additional credibility per se.

The analysis in *Community Health Systems* likely succeeded because its false claims allegations, that CHS defrauded Medicare, were supported by a complete set of available Medicare billing claims. There was little room to argue, for example, that the relator's analysis was unrepresentative of CHS claims. The relators in *Community Health Systems* could point to how CHS defrauded Medicare, and how the data supported such assertion. The weakness of CFI's analysis in *Victaulic Co.* is not that CFI used eBay. Rather, the weakness is that CFI assumed eBay data was representative of Victaulic's sales of pipe fittings in the United States. Had CFI identified specific shipments which were incorrectly labeled and then put on eBay, or had CFI demonstrated that eBay was representative of Victaulic's US sales, CFI's statistical and data analysis would have been stronger.

For these and other false claims cases, Big Data is a useful tool. However, litigants need to clearly demonstrate that their results are no mere hiccup or accident of numbers, but part of a deliberate fraudulent scheme.

Financial Fraud Allegations and Big Data Analytics

Certain types of litigation in the financial industry also lend themselves quite well to Big Data analytics techniques and methodologies. Financial claims involving company stock prices are especially good examples and have a relatively long history. In these types of cases, it is often alleged that statements made by company executives, or information not disclosed by company executives, resulted in a reduction in the value of the company that ultimately hurt the economic well-being of shareholders. Large collections of financial data, including information such as stock prices, news reports, and accounting data, are used in analyses in these types of cases to determine if the information or omission of information actually had an impact on the company's stock price and then the information is used separately to determine the size of the economic loss incurred by shareholders.

Specifically, the Securities and Exchange Act of 1934, 10b-5, makes it unlawful for any person to use deceptive practices or make misleading statements in the purchase or sale of any security. Ultimately, the Supreme Court adopted a presumption of reliance, which states that investors rely on a company's statements when deciding to purchase a security. This presumption of reliance adopted by the court is based on the "fraud-on-the-market theory," which is the belief that security prices reflect all publicly available information. Investors, attempting to earn a profit by market trading, will utilize every useful piece of data. When new information hits the market, it changes the total composition of information available to investors about the given securities. Prices will then adjust quickly to reflect the market's new valuation of a security.

Assuming capital markets are efficient, a company's stock price should fall in response to bad news and a company's stock price should rise in response to good news. A misrepresentation or omission, therefore, prevents a security's price from adjusting to where the market would set the real value. An investor is then caught by surprise if a company fraudulently misrepresented itself, and garners a loss when the price of the security adjusts to account for the alleged fraud.

When alleged misrepresentations occur, they have the effect of either inflating a company's stock price or maintaining the stock prices at an artificially high level. When the misrepresentation is later revealed, this is called a "corrective disclosure." Corrective disclosures often have the effect of depressing a company's stock price, because they tend to conceal bad (rather than good) news.

How then can the vast amount of data on security's prices, market analyses, and company information be distilled to determine if a company's misrepresentations significantly impacted the price of its stock?

The most common answer is the event study. An event study is a statistical method which measures the effects of an economic event on the value of a firm. The event study is used in a variety of fields to study how a variety of firm-specific events impact a company's securities price. This would include mergers or acquisitions, earnings announcements, or issues of new debt or equity. Event studies are also used by economists to measure how changes in the macroeconomic or regulatory environment impact a firm. But, event studies have also been used to evaluate how fraudulent misrepresentations impact a company's stock price.

To measure how a specific event impacts a security's price, an event study must disentangle a company's security from general market trends. If a company's stock price increased, and the market also increased, then the stock's price rise can be explained by broad movements in the market. However, a security is also affected by industry-specific information. If a company in the electronics sector saw its stock price decline one day, while the market increased, that could be viewed as unusual. But suppose all securities in the electronics sector declined the same day, then the company's stock price decline can be explained by a movement in the electronics industry.

In an event study, calculations are based on the "excess returns" of a security. The statistical method used to calculate a security's excess return filters out price changes in the market around a security and conceptually allows the analyst to analyze the impact of the new market information. Once this dataset of excess returns is constructed, an event study will then examine specific dates, or groups of dates, when a relevant event occurred. For example, if a company released a corrective disclosure on Monday, what happened to the stock price? An event study will test to see if the rise or fall in the stock price is so far outside of the expected range that it is statistically unlikely that random chance alone would have generated the stock price outcome.

Courts have recognized the utility of event studies for their role in disentangling complex data and information on which markets value publicly traded securities. Speaking on the use of such data and statistics for securities fraud, the Northern District Court of California in 2007 commented:

> Use of an event study or similar analysis is necessary more accurately to [sic] isolate the influences of information specific to [the company] which defendants allegedly have distorted.

One of the most important securities fraud cases in the past decade was *Erica P. John Fund v. Halliburton*. This case has a long history of complex legal appeals and went to the Supreme Court twice in the suit's 16-year history. Much of the case turned on the data analytics and the resulting case law that was created from the many rulings in the case has a significant impact on how Big Data analytics are performed in litigation.

In this case the plaintiffs, who were holders of Halliburton stock between 1999 and 2001, alleged Halliburton and its executives intentionally misled investors and, as a result, inflated Halliburton's share price. The alleged misrepresentations included accounting rules violations, publishing misleading reports on the company's acquisition of a competing firm, and understating Halliburton's liabilities in a pending asbestos litigation. The case raised fundamental questions on the importance of the efficient market hypothesis, the evidence of price impact, the definition of material misrepresentation, and the information contained in securities prices. The case, which was first filed in 2002, finally reached a $100 million settlement agreement in 2018.

For the plaintiff class and the defendants, *Halliburton* centered on a crucial element: could the plaintiffs prove that Halliburton's alleged misrepresentations and false statements impacted the price of Halliburton's stock? Could the defense rebut such allegations and demonstrate these price movements could not have been the result of such alleged "misrepresentations"?

Background

Halliburton was a publicly traded energy services and construction company based out of Houston, Texas, with an annual revenue of $12 billion in 2000 (the middle of the plaintiffs' class period). In 1998, Halliburton announced it would acquire its competitor, Dresser, in a $7 billion deal. In mid-1998, Halliburton stock traded for as high as $56 per share, but fell by the end of the year. The plaintiffs' lawsuit alleged that Halliburton's executives actively misrepresented the true nature of Halliburton's financial health in a number of different ways. Plaintiffs alleged that through accounting sleight of hand, Halliburton hide certain cost and cost overruns from investors. Additionally, plaintiffs alleged that Halliburton significantly overstated the revenue that the company would receive from the acquisition of its competing company, Dresser. Finally, the plaintiffs alleged that the executive team at Halliburton allegedly did not pass on the full extent of its asbestos liability to investors. During the first half of 2000, the plaintiffs contended that all of these issues were not disclosed to investors, and instead Halliburton continued to sound positive assurances to financial markets.

For much of the class period, Halliburton stock traded between $30 and $50 per share, reaching as high as $55.18 per share. By January 2002, Halliburton stock traded at a low of $8.60 per share, a 15-year low for the company. The plaintiffs contended that this large decline over a two-year period resulted after the true state of the company was revealed to investors. In 2002, a securities fraud class action lawsuit was filed on behalf of investors against Halliburton. The complaint alleged that the company inflated its stock price between September 1, 1998, and January 15, 2002. Both the plaintiffs and the defendant retained expert witnesses, who employed different event study methodologies to determine if Halliburton's "corrective disclosures" materially impacted Halliburton's stock price.

The experts for both the plaintiffs and the defense used a standardized approach to answer questions about price impact. Event studies require data on the company's stock before, during, and after the class period, data which is readily available. The New York Stock Exchange (NYSE), for example, maintains historical datasets on all of its publicly traded securities, which can be downloaded after paying for a subscription.

Since Halliburton had a publicly traded stock during the class period, the stock's price, trading volume, turnover rates could be readily obtained from places like the NYSE; information on the company's market capitalization, public offerings, and investors could also be obtained from analyst reports, market research firms, or the company's filings with the Securities and Exchange Commission (SEC). Data on similar corporate stocks and market indices are also widely available for thousands of securities traded on the open market. Both sides utilized these resources. Ultimately, the data in this case was extensive.

After determining the "event window" and collecting market data, both the plaintiff and defense experts constructed their control or peer indices of companies similar to Halliburton. These indices control for stock price movements in the market, so the study could determine how company-specific information impacted Halliburton stock.

In this case, the plaintiff and defense analysts differed on the size and scope of Halliburton's market. It is unsurprising, therefore, that they used different methods to determine Halliburton's industry peers.

According to the plaintiff analysis, a company was considered similar if it was listed on at least four relevant energy services indexes, and if the company was mentioned as a competitor or comparable to Halliburton in published financial analysts' reports, such as those published by Moody's and other stock valuation and analysis organizations. In contrast, the defendant's expert report constructed their peer group of companies based on the S&P 500 Energy Index and the Energy and Construction companies in the Fortune 1000 index known as the Fortune E&C index.

After constructing all of these indices, the defense and plaintiff experts' reports used various statistical techniques to construct the "predicted returns" of Halliburton's stock over the class period and the stock's "excess returns."

The final datasets which each analyst used for their event study, these "excess returns" of Halliburton stock, were based wholly on the peer index they created, which, of course, was different for each analyst. As a result, and unsurprisingly, each analyst reached quite different conclusions.

Findings

The analysts in this report supported the plaintiffs' claim that Halliburton investors were misled and, as a result, suffered economic damages due to the company withholding vital information on its financial health. The report argued that had Halliburton reported its operational problems and the full extent of its asbestos liability far earlier, then the company's stock price would have declined before the class period. The plaintiffs used the report to argue for class certification.

In contrast to the plaintiffs' first expert report, the defense's expert report found no price impact from any of the plaintiffs' alleged misrepresentations. Their analyst reviewed 35 separate dates on which the plaintiffs alleged that misrepresentations or corrective disclosures occurred. The defense event study found that Halliburton's stock had a statistically significant price movement on only one day, December 7, 2001. Relying on their expert's data analysis, the defense argued that the court should deny class certification. The defendant's data showed that, on all 35 dates mentioned either in the plaintiffs' complaint or in the plaintiffs' first expert report, there was no evidence of price impact.

At this stage, it's important to note how subtle differences in basic assumptions can potentially lead to different results. *Erica P. John Fund v Halliburton* had a complex legal history, of which the plaintiff and defense experts' reports represented just one part of a 16-year case. However, the data and evidence presented by both parties was crucial in several rulings.

Lessons

In 2008, the District Court initially refused class certification on grounds unrelated to price impact (loss causation). The Fifth Circuit Court of Appeals agreed, saying the plaintiffs' evidence did not show any loss from fraudulent activity. The Supreme Court vacated and remanded the case (*Halliburton I*), arguing that securities fraud plaintiffs did not need to prove loss causation in order to obtain class certification. The Supreme Court again ruled on the case in 2014 (known as *Halliburton II*) and again remanded the case, declaring that the plaintiffs also did not need to show price impact for class certification, but that defendants could present their own evidence of a lack of price impact at the class certification stage.

Finally, on July 25, 2015, the District Court granted the plaintiffs' motion for class certification, but only for those who held Halliburton stock on December 7, 2001, the single day with the largest stock price decline. In its judgment, the District Court borrowed elements from all three event studies, and ultimately determined that Halliburton could not refute lack of price impact for December 7, 2001.

On February 21, 2017, the parties reached a preliminary settlement agreement. Halliburton agreed to pay the class members $100,000,000; in exchange, Halliburton would forgo admitting guilt and any liability rising from the plaintiffs' claims of fraud. The court granted preliminary approval, and by 2018 the case had finally resolved itself in the federal court.

The various court rulings in the case clearly show that in securities litigation, Big Data and analytical techniques are essential components. Litigants compete to provide the most persuasive evidence of price impact (or lack thereof) before a judge, particularly at class certification. The more coherent and rigorous a given analytical approach, the more likely it is to withstand a challenge.

Discrimination Allegations and Big Data Analytics: *Miami v. Bank of America*

Introduction

The Fair Housing Act of 1968 prohibits housing discrimination on account of race, religion, sex, national origin, familial status, or disability. The legislation addresses discrimination when renting or buying a home, getting a mortgage, seeking housing assistance, and so on. The enactment of the Fair Housing Act (FHA) addressed specific discriminatory practices like redlining, whereby landlords, homeowners, communities, and lending institutions refused to offer housing or credit to members of racial minorities. The FHA also addresses what is referred to as "reverse redlining," that is, the practice of extending credit to protected class borrowers on unequal terms. Litigation involving lending has a long history of utilizing Big Data analytics.

The FHA established a two-track system of enforcement. Individuals believed to be suffering from discrimination can file a complaint with the Department of Housing and Urban Development (HUD); if the allegations are credible, the Department of Justice opens up a criminal suit. Individuals, deemed an "aggrieved person," are also licensed to bring civil suits against housing and loan providers for discriminatory practices, and are eligible to recover damages.

Civil rights litigation, particularly in labor law, comprises two different theories of discrimination: disparate treatment and disparate impact. Disparate treatment is intentional, explicit discrimination against a protected class on account of race, sex, and so on. For example, a broker refusing to sell or show a home to prospective buyers of a given racial minority is disparate treatment.

Disparate impact, however, is subtle or even unintentional discrimination against a protected class. A policy or practice which on the surface appears to be neutral but disproportionately impacts members of a protected class is defined as disparate impact. For example, a bank offering mortgages to only applicants with a perfect credit score would have disparate impact, as racial minorities tend to have lower credit scores than their White counterparts. Disparate impact in and of itself was not illegal. A policy causing disparate impact becomes discriminatory if the employer cannot justify the necessity of the employment practice.

Disparate impact emerged as a doctrine in federal law following *Griggs v. Duke Power Co.*, decided in 1971. The suit, an employment discrimination case, considered whether additional educational requirements for a job duty, which had no relation to a person's ability to perform a job, were discriminatory toward Black employees. The court ruled that policies which had an "adverse impact" on hiring, which disproportionately impacted racial minorities, had to be justified and reasonably related to job duties.

For a while, federal court precedent was unclear on whether disparate impact theory applied to housing discrimination and the practices mentioned in the Fair Housing Act. Federal Circuit court precedents largely agreed that disparate impact claims were cognizable, within the court's jurisdiction, under the FHA as early as 1977 in *Metro. House. Dev. Corp. v. Arlington Heights*. In *Texas Department of Housing and Community Affairs v. The Inclusive Communities Project, Inc.*, decided in 2015, the court held that Congress did indeed intend to allow disparate impact claims under the FHA. In the ruling, the court held that, for a suit by the plaintiff to succeed, they had to prove a policy by the defendant caused a racial disparity. The ruling set new precedents for potential plaintiffs filing civil suits:

> Particular emphasis was placed on a "robust causality requirement" which requires plaintiffs who bring disparate impact claims based on statistical disparities to (1) identify the defendant's policy or policies causing that disparity, noting that "one-time decisions that may not be a policy at all;" and (2) produce statistical evidence at the pleading stage demonstrating that a defendant's policy or policies cause that disparity.[4]

Here, proof of disparate impact now had to provide concrete statistical evidence of the defendant's policies causing disparate impact. At the convergence suits under the FHA and the use of Big Data are a series of lawsuits filed by cities against major banks and mortgage brokers after the 2008 recession. These suites started before, but were influenced by, the ruling in *Texas Department of Housing and Community Affairs v. Inclusive Communities Project, Inc.* These lawsuits alleged that certain banks denied minority applicants better loan conditions (redlining), or offering high-

[4] *Texas Dept. of Housing and Community Affairs v. Inclusive Communities Project, Inc.*, 576 U.S. 135 S. CT 507 (2015).

interest mortgages to minority applicants (reverse redlining); the result is that many minority homeowners went into foreclosure when the US housing market collapsed, which allegedly damaged several cities' finances.

In 2013 the City of Miami filed an FHA suit against three major US banks: Citibank, Wells Fargo, and Bank of America, alleging the banks enabled discriminatory lending practices which violated the FHA. All three suits allege the same practices and share a similar case history. For expediency, *Miami v. Bank of America* epitomizes all three cases neatly. The City of Miami alleged that Bank of America, through its subsidiary Countrywide Financial, deliberately and arbitrarily targeted high-interest-rate home mortgages to Miami's African-American and Hispanic population before the 2008 recession. It is alleged that these high-interest mortgages caused foreclosure rates to rise, and, as Miami claimed, led to lost tax revenue and increased spending on municipal services.

Bank of America was adamant that did not cause higher foreclosure rates; rather, many borrowers went into default for reasons other than the company's mortgages. Rather, Bank of America claimed it was being unfairly targeted by the city as the cause of Miami's economic downturn. The *Miami v. Bank of America* raised questions of who can file a suit under the FHA, disparate impact, and what constitutes the proximate cause of a perceived discriminatory practice. The case reached the Supreme Court in 2016, and in 2017 was remanded back to the Eleventh Court for additional litigation. As of 2019, the Eleventh Circuit authorized the City of Miami's lawsuit to proceed.

Background

In 2013, Bank of America was a national banking conglomerate headquartered out of Charlotte, North Carolina, with sub-branches specializing in different financial services. In 2012, the company recorded an income of over $4 billion. Bank of America (BoA) is considered one of the "Big Four" major banks in the United States, alongside Citigroup, Wells Fargo, and JP Morgan Chase. In 2008, Bank of America acquired Countrywide Financial Corporation (CFC) and its subsidiaries, Countrywide Home Loans, Inc. (CHL) and Countrywide Bank (CWB), which became the Bank of America Home Loans division of the company. These institutions created, authorized, and financed Countrywide's mortgage and home loan lending practices, later subsumed by Bank of America.

The plaintiffs alleged that Countrywide, and its successor Bank of America, engaged in several business practices which, while facially neutral, led to minority borrowers being issued loans at higher rates than similarly situated White borrowers.

As an example, the complaint reviews Countrywide's lending practices from 2004 up until its acquisition by Bank of America. Countrywide both directly underwrote mortgages to borrowers as well as to wholesale brokerages. In both of these lending practices, the company utilized a two-stage decision-making process when setting the terms and conditions of a loan for a borrower.

In the first stage, Countrywide set the base price of mortgages and home loan products by utilizing objective criteria which measured the credit worthiness of an applicant. These base prices could be adjusted to account for market conditions and the loan's worth to potential investors. In the second stage, Countrywide allowed its retail mortgage loan officers (or the wholesale broker) to adjust the final loan price charged to borrowers above or below the base price of the loan. Employees and brokers could alter the standard fees and closing costs. Though the company provided no clear guidance on how such adjustments should be made, it actively incentivized employees and brokers to raise prices. Countrywide provided additional compensation to employees and brokers if the final price of the loan was above the base price (known as an "outage"). In addition, Countrywide had a system to flag applicants eligible for lower risk products, but there was no requirement to inform the applicant of potentially better terms.

The plaintiff alleged that BoA, before and after acquiring Countrywide, assumed its own facially neutral but discriminatory lending practices. The City of Miami supported this claim through three confidential witnesses, all former mortgage loan officers who worked at Bank of America. All three alleged several predatory business practices which intentionally targeted minorities, including steering minority borrowers into riskier loans. One of the confidential witnesses stated that:

> "interest only" and "pick-a-payment" loans were popular in Miami, and [the witness] understood that borrowers were approved for such loans based on repayment of interest payments alone – not interest and principal. In [the witness'] experience, few of the borrowers were able to pay down the loan principal on these loans along with interest every month. "After four or five years, that's how everything went the way it did," [the witness] said. "They

> couldn't afford it. Half the time they couldn't even afford the (full) interest on these homes." BoA paid its employees more for steering minorities into predatory loans.

The witnesses alleged that BoA steered its loan officers away from offering loans which were more beneficial to low-income buyers (such as CRA, Community Reinvestment Act, loan) and instead offered employees higher commissions on riskier loans. Additional fees loan officers charged were often not disclosed to applicants and, in the witness' words, often eluded notice by minority borrowers.

Most often, the witnesses asserted that BoA marketed loans with low teaser rates (referred to as "pick-your-payment" loans) to borrowers from predominantly minority neighborhoods, without considering the ability of such borrowers to repay these loans once interest rates rose. The result is that many low teaser rate loans went into delinquency, default, and foreclosure. This, Miami claimed, proved Bank of America engaged in reverse redlining: contributing to the high rates of foreclosure in the city's predominantly minority neighborhoods.

Once minority homeowners found themselves in difficulty, BoA actively induced foreclosures by refusing to refinance or make modifications to existing loans. One of the confidential witnesses claimed that, between 2011 and 2013, BoA did not offer regular refinancing on mortgages at over 80% of the value of a house. Most mortgages at over 80% of a home's value were on teaser rates, and many such borrowers were either African-American or Hispanic. This, the city asserted, was proof that Bank of America actively encouraged foreclosures on minority-owned properties.

Bank of America's response was multifaceted. Specifically addressing the claim of disparate impact, the defense argued that the city's claims fell short, because it could not point to any specific terms or conditions of alleged discriminatory mortgages it offered. Bank of America argued that the company's loan terms and conditions could not be causally linked to foreclosures. Rather, the defense asserted the evidence showed that borrower-specific and macroeconomic factors caused most foreclosures at the time.

> In 2009, the Vice-Chair of the Miami City Commission specifically admitted that "[p]eople are walking away from [their loans] 'cause they can't afford it anymore, and it's all based on the tough economy that we're facing."

> … many borrowers have self-reported that these exact issues were the reasons they sought loan modifications, with the single most-reported reason being income loss. Notably, the unemployment rate, and specifically the Miami unemployment rate, skyrocketed during the period of time in question. And, defaults occur across all mortgage loan types, including prime loans, and not just among particular loan products.

Nor does the city, the defense asserted, mention the hundreds of thousands of loans made by other lenders in Miami at the time. Bank of America was just one lender, and of all the reasons that could plausibly be linked to increased foreclosure rates, the City of Miami deliberately chose to argue Bank of America engaged in discriminatory lending.

The defense argued that the city's lawsuit, similar to other lawsuits against mortgage lenders at the time, was based on speculative inferences connecting alleged injuries to asserted wrongful conduct. Thus, the city's causal chain of events was broken. BoA further argued that even if Miami had higher foreclosure rates, the foreclosures could not be causally linked to losses in property taxes and increased spending on vacant properties. Therefore, the plaintiff could not sufficiently prove it suffered an injury. The plaintiff, according to the defense, could not also prove such injury was caused by Bank of America's practices, which meant they could not argue a disparate impact claim under the FHA.

In *Miami v. Bank of America*, the city had to demonstrate that Bank of America's practices not only resulted in a disparate impact, but that BoA's lending practices was the proximate cause of the city's alleged injury. The City of Miami thus employed a statistical analysis to attempt to link racial disparities in borrowing terms to racial disparities in foreclosure rates in Miami. The defense wanted to refute these allegations and demonstrate that higher rates of foreclosures on BoA loans were not due to discriminatory lending, but other factors. The defense retained its own expert witnesses.

Data

How did the City of Miami and Bank of America approach the disparate impact claim?

Both sides utilized home mortgage data from Bank of America (and Countrywide) made available by the Home Mortgage Disclosure Act (HMDA) of 1975. The HMDA required that mortgage lenders maintain, and disclose to the government, information on home loans they originated, including the loan amount, the home's location, the borrower's race, the borrower's income, and others. In 2017, 6762 lenders were required to report their mortgage loan histories under the HMDA, which reported over 16.3 million loan records. These are very voluminous files.

Historical HMDA data is publicly available through the Federal Financial Institutions Examination Council (FFIEC). Both sides had access to Bank of America's mortgage data between 2004 and 2012, as well as mortgage data for census tracts within Miami. Both the City of Miami and Bank of America utilized summary statistics within the city limits to construct their cases.

The City of Miami also employed this data to construct statistical models to determine if race was an important predictor of several factors in Bank of America's mortgage data. To support the allegations of reverse redlining, the city examined if there were racial disparities in loans originated by Bank of America which they deemed "predatory." Predatory loans were defined as high-cost, subprime, interest-only, balloon payment, negative amortization, no documentation, and adjustable rate mortgage loans.

The city's statistical models controlled for factors such as the borrower's race, credit history, loan-to-value ratio, loan-to-income ratio, and other loan-specific factors. Using Bank of America's data, the City of Miami also constructed a separate analysis to determine if a borrower's race was an important predictor for foreclosed properties.

The City of Miami then constructed separate odds ratios that showed the relative likelihood that a given person would receive a high-interest loan. Were African-American or Hispanic borrowers more, equally, or less likely to receive a high-interest loan than White borrowers? Were African-American or Hispanic borrowers more, equally, or less likely to be foreclosed on than White borrowers? Were these differences statistically significant?

Findings

According to the plaintiff, their analysis showed that minorities in Miami received predatory loan terms from Bank of America more frequently than their peers. An African-American borrower was 1.6 times more likely than a similarly situated White borrower to receive a high-interest loan. Similarly, a Latino borrower was 2.1 times more likely than a similarly situated White borrower to receive a high-interest loan. Such disparities persisted even among borrowers with good credit. African-American borrowers with FICO credit scores above 660 were 1.533 times more likely to receive a high-interest loan than similarly situated White borrowers, while Latino borrowers with FICO scores above 660 were 2.137 times more likely to receive a high-interest loan than similarly situated White borrowers.

The plaintiff took the additional step of examining the racial composition of Miami's neighborhoods, to see if there were correlations between neighborhoods and predatory loans. A borrower in a census tract where 90% of households were African-American or Latino were 1.585 times more likely to receive a predatory loan than a similar borrower in a census tract where at least 50% of the households were White. These numbers, the plaintiff opined, were statistically significant. Miami also provided a map of the city, showing the geographic distribution of predatory loans and the racial composition of neighborhoods. The map illustrates that predatory loans issued by BoA were disproportionately concentrated in minority neighborhoods. To further illustrate the point, the plaintiff pointed out that between 2004 and 2012, 21.9% of BoA loans made to African-American or Latino borrowers in Miami were high cost, but only 8.9% made to White borrowers were high cost.

The analysis demonstrated that a predatory loan was 1.7 times more likely to be foreclosed on than a prime loan. In addition, a predatory loan made to an African-American borrower was 2.7 times more likely to be foreclosed on than that made to a similarly situated White borrower with similar characteristics. A Latino borrower with a predatory loan was 2.7 times more likely to be foreclosed upon than a similarly situated White borrower with similar characteristics. The plaintiff argued that these calculations supported its claim that Bank of America engaged in lending activities which caused disparate impact that violated the Fair Housing Act.

The defense retained two experts who submitted the report: one of the defense's experts utilized the HMDA data. This report supplied by the defendant argued that it was unrealistically narrow for the city to claim that specific loan products or terms were the sole or even primary cause of foreclosures. Instead, the main factor causing foreclosures, the report argued, is declining home prices. Plenty of borrowers had negative or insufficient equity in their homes when prices declined, and opted to default rather than continue paying their mortgages. Additionally, the 2008 recession caused plenty of borrowers to become unemployed or lose a portion of their income. The report argued that Miami was particularly hard hit, as unemployment peaked at 12.5% of the labor force in March 2010. Plenty of borrowers facing foreclosure listed a curtailment of income as the primary reason for their hardship. To further support this claim, the report cites that defaults increased across all loan categories after 2006, not just "predatory loans" the city cited.

The defense report examined the combined data from Bank of America and Countrywide loans in Miami, as defined by census tracts, between 2004 and 2011. Examining the HMDA data, the report first pointed out that, at most, BoA made up only 11.18% of all mortgages in Miami during this period. Rather, the mortgage market was dominated by other lenders. In addition, the report asserted that Bank of America did not make a disproportionate number of loans to minorities in Miami. In census tracts where minorities made up >80% of the population, Bank of America and Countrywide made up only 13.36% of the loans, hardly out of line with their market share or evidence of targeting minorities.

The defense report further asserted that BoA did not make up a disproportionate number of high-priced loans between 2004 and 2011; rather, the HMDA data showed that combined, BoA made up a small share of high-priced loans in minority-majority census tracts in Miami. Only 18.6% of Bank of America and Countrywide mortgages in minority-majority census tracts were high-priced loans, compared to 34.97% of mortgages made by other lenders. For census tracts where minorities made up >80% of the population, just 23.19% of Bank of America and Countrywide loans in these tracts were high-priced loans, compared to an average of 40.9% of loans made by other lenders.

The defense argued that the data did not suggest that BoA engaged in a pattern of predatory lending. Rather, the data from Miami seem to show quite the opposite: that compared to other lenders, Bank of America was relatively restrained in issuing high-priced mortgages in Miami. Finally, the defense report commented on the unusual circumstances of Miami's housing market. Using census data, the defense's report notes that, of Miami's 80 census tracts, only 4 were majority White. This meant that comparing minority and White mortgage lending in the city was both impractical and illogical, since the sample sizes were completely disproportionate and biased any results. In addition, a large proportion of mortgages in Miami at the time originated for non-owners. Between 2004 and 2011, 29.2% of all home loans (not just from BoA) were investment or second homes, which compared to 13.9% of mortgages nationwide. As investment properties are highly sensitive to fluctuations in house prices, the defense report asserts, when the housing market in Miami plummeted, these properties were most likely to default and foreclosed on.

This evidence, the defense argued, supported the claim that Bank of America did not engage in reverse redlining or predatory lending activities. The city's claim that BoA's activities were the cause of the city's lost revenue and increased spending on public services, due to increased vacancies and foreclosures, was thus implausible.

With all this evidence in hand, it was up to the court to decide if the city's complaint was compelling enough to continue to trial.

Lessons

The District Court in July 2014 granted the defendant's motion to dismiss on several grounds. Speaking to the data analysis itself, the court was unpersuaded. It found that the plaintiff could not properly establish proximate cause: that the defendant's alleged redlining and reverse redlining caused the city injury. The city appealed the dismissal to the Eleventh Circuit. The Eleventh Circuit, taking up the appeal of the case, concluded that the District Court overstepped.

While the Eleventh Circuit agreed any number of confounding variables could muddle a determination if BoA engaged in discriminatory lending practices, the court ruled the city's alleged chain of causation was perfectly plausible. The city's statistical analyses could link BoA's treatment of minority borrowers to foreclosures. At such an early stage, the city's standing to sue, the court ruled, was both plausible and sufficient to proceed. Of particular note is the Eleventh Circuit's attitude toward the city's analysis. The court stressed that its opinion was not passing judgment on the ultimate success or failure of the city's claim, but the results were enough to say the city adequately pled its case at this stage.

The case was appealed to the Supreme Court, which ruled in October 2016. The majority concluded the city did have standing to sue, as the Fair Housing Act granted a wide zone of interest for aggrieved parties. The Supreme Court remanded the case back to the Eleventh Circuit for further deliberation to determine if there was "some direct relation" to Bank of America's activities and the city's claims of lost tax revenue under the FHA.

In May 2019, the Eleventh Circuit concluded there was some direct relation between the city's injury and BoA's conduct. In it writings, the

Eleventh Circuit extensively cited the plaintiff's statistical analyses in its overview of the case, constantly reiterating their findings. By contrast, the defendant's reports, other than the broad assertions, were not cited as extensively. The defense did not challenge the plaintiff's statistical analysis, only offering broad conclusions which drew attention to other factors. For example, the defense did not directly refute the plaintiff's data showing African-American borrowers obtained more high-interest loans than White borrowers. Once more, the Eleventh Circuit remanded the case for further proceedings. Litigation is ongoing as of the writing of this book.

Miami v. Bank of America demonstrates the power of more complex statistical techniques using Big Data. Despite the complications in calculating odds ratios, the courts, particularly the Eleventh Circuit, interpreted the results without confusion. Again, the case demonstrates the various evidentiary standards which litigants must navigate when utilizing data-based evidence.

Online Advertising Fraud

The nature of online advertising is essentially an enormous and Big Data-driven activity with millions of impressions per second. These impressions are in turn used as a basis for ads being sold to businesses. More impressions, equal all other things, translate to a higher price. Online advertising is an enormous sector. Globally, it is estimated that in 2019 expenditures on online advertising will be $330 billion. In the United States, online advertising is estimated to reach nearly $130 billion in 2019.[5] The sector involves multiple parties spread around the globe and complex technology and Big Data, which includes generating 4000–10,000 ad impressions per day per person in the United States.[6] With increased complexity of any activity comes an increased probability of fraudulent or other illegal behavior.

An example of the congruence of Big Data analytics, the internet economy, and the US legal system is *Pulaski & Middleman, LLC v Google*, a civil class action based on Google's online advertising practices. The class, a group of businesses which paid for advertisements online, alleged that Google misrepresented where advertisers' ads would appear on the web. The class claimed they paid Google, unknowingly, for ad space on blank

[5] eMarketer, Digital Ad Spending 2019, March 2019.
[6] Ibid.

or phony websites without the advertisers' knowledge. Google defended its actions and asserted its conduct in placing advertisements was not unlawful or actionable. Furthermore, Google asserted the ads on these blank domains were, actually, as noticed as much as ads on real websites.

The class, which was composed of businesses that paid for the use of Google's AdWords program between 2004 and 2008, sued for violations of California's Business and Professions Code. *Pulaski & Middleman, LLC v Google* raised fundamental questions of what constitutes fraudulent activity, litigation of state law in federal courts, and the certification of class actions in the wake of recent case law precedent. The case, which was first filed in 2008, went before the Ninth Circuit and was settled for $22.5 million in 2017.

Importantly, the case involved the use of Big Data to conceptualize both liability and potential damages. The Google AdWords litigation is a signpost to the future uses of Big Data analytics and expert witness evidence.

Background

Google is the world's largest online advertiser, heavily linked with its search engine www.google.com. In 2009 Google's revenue totaled $23.6 billion. Over 97% of Google's revenue between 2005 and 2009 was from advertising, specifically customers paying Google and website partners for delivering and hosting advertisements. Advertisers pay through Google's AdWords program, which is an auction-based advertising system which began in October 2000. Advertisers bid for particular search terms, which determine the placement of their ads on the search engine. The more an advertiser bids, the better their placement of the given ad.

Google also had a program for website publishers called AdSense, where advertisers' ads would be placed. Revenue from advertisements published through AdSense accounted for 35–44% of Google's revenue. According to the plaintiffs, Google matched ads to network pages using its own algorithms. Google's search algorithms determined the most relevant placement matches given an ad's keywords and search terms.

According to the plaintiffs, the AdSense program included inactive domains which did not have actual content and error pages. One of the named plaintiffs calculated that 16.4% of their total pay-per-click bill came from such pages. The plaintiffs contended that, as advertisers, Google did not inform them that their advertisements were being displayed on these types of domains. Rather, the plaintiffs contend that Google misled advertisers, by claiming that these programs applied rigorous standards when monitoring the websites and products displayed in its advertising services. Google, the plaintiffs asserted, made assurances that ads would be targeted on sites which were contextually relevant, placed near contextually relevant content appropriate for the ad. In addition, the plaintiffs contended that Google designed its programs in such a way that it was impossible to opt out of including advertisements on pages that need not have actual content. The plaintiffs contended they were injured because advertisers would have opted out of lower quality domains.

At the early stage of the case, one central issue was whether the plaintiff class met all the requirements to certify as a class. The plaintiffs had to demonstrate to the court that common questions of liability and restitution predominated over individual claims. This was complicated by the varying nature of Google's advertising program, since individual companies placed separate bids for separate ad space at separate times.

Could the plaintiffs devise a workable methodology to calculate damages for class members? How could the defense illustrate that alleged damages from online advertising were too varied to be considered as a whole class? Both sides retained expert witnesses to assist in answering this central question.

Data

The data used to answer questions of liability and damages in this case was of course the data generated by Google. Neither side challenged the accuracy or reliability of Google's AdWords program data.

The plaintiffs' first set of information requests, or interrogatories, asked Google for conversion rates for all clicks on advertisements between 2004 and 2009. An ad's conversion rate measures how likely a click on a page will convert into an action the advertiser wants. This data would allow the plaintiffs to evaluate whether ads placed on error pages were less effective than regular web domains. The plaintiffs also asked for specific data regarding every advertisement placed on domains that did not have actual content or were error pages.

Google expressed privacy concerns releasing both its data and its exact auction pricing methodology. The defense asserted that public disclosure of such data would cause Google economic harm by giving third parties and potential competitors access to sensitive and internal information that

Google has developed for its own use as part of its business operations, relating to conversions and clicks associated with its AdWords program. As a result of protective orders in the case, most of the expert reports and data citations are redacted or sealed from public access. The data requests from interrogatories are public record and discussions of expert witness reports summarize their findings.

Findings

In *Pulaski & Middleman, LLC v. Google*, the questions turned less on the data itself rather than the data's potential utility for determining common damages. The plaintiffs' primary expert filed two reports which outlined three methods for measuring restitution. The expert's reports attempted to persuade the court to grant class certification, on the grounds that common damages could be derived from a class action.

The plaintiffs' expert concluded that damages for the class could be calculated using conservative but reliable methods which compare the actual prices paid by advertisers against the estimated prices advertisers would have paid had Google informed the class some ads were placed on error pages and parked domains. The plaintiffs' expert presented three different approaches as to how economic damages could be calculated. The defense submitted a variety of expert reports and testimony to refute the plaintiffs' expert, in order to persuade the court that a common methodology for damages was impossible for the case.

Lessons

In January of 2012, the District Court issued a judgment in which it denied class certification for the suit. The court found the plaintiffs met the requirements to certify a class based on numerosity, commonality, typicality, and adequacy. However, the court ruled the calculation of damages for the plaintiffs would require highly individual inquiries and it is therefore not suitable for class treatment. The court cited that the highly complex nature of the AdWords auction process generates separate costs for individual advertisers for every ad.

The plaintiffs appealed the ruling to the Ninth Circuit, which heard arguments in 2014 and issued its judgment in September 2015. The Ninth Circuit reversed the District Court's denial of class certification, and remanded the case for further proceedings. The Ninth Circuit found that the District Court erred in its judgment by not correctly applying its past precedent which stated that differing damage calculations alone could not defeat class certification. Furthermore, it did not find the plaintiffs' damages methodologies complex or arbitrary enough to defeat class certification. For the Ninth Circuit, damages could feasibly and efficiently be calculated once liability had been adjudicated.

The case, upon remand from the Ninth Circuit, continued as if the class had been certified. In the two years following the ruling, both sides agreed to mediation. In February 2017, *Pulaski & Middleman, LLC v. Google* reached a settlement agreement in which Google agreed to pay the class $22.5 million. Since the case settled, the plaintiffs' damages calculations under the three different models were not necessary; but, based on the plaintiffs' estimates, complete restitution to the class would have totaled between $45 and $77 million had they won at trial.

The District Court and the Ninth Circuit differed in their opinions as to how complicated the damages calculations would have been, had the case proceeded. Based on the differing datasets and information available, would damages have been difficult to construct? In a Big Data analysis, large data merges pose a significant but not insurmountable problem. Arriving at the most precise calculations would have required the appropriate merger of at least four data sources.

First, the plaintiff class' entire payment history under the AdWords program, during the class period, which could potentially be a massive dataset in and of itself. Within this data, links to error pages and no content domains would have to be flagged in order to calculate plaintiffs' damages. This would necessitate some list of parked domains and error pages to match to the plaintiffs' payments. Next, advertisers would have to determine what they would have actually bid for ad space if they had known certain clicks would be due to no content sites. Finally, calculating damages under the most complex scenarios would require a proxy for Google's AdWords auction algorithm (which Google would most likely not be willing to provide), which would have to determine what the plaintiffs would have paid given their adjusted bids. With this combined dataset, damages could be calculated by simply subtracting what the plaintiffs actually paid from what the plaintiffs would have paid "but for" Google's omissions.

Pulaski & Middleman, LLC v. Google case, which ran from 2008 to 2017, is still on the cutting edge of internet and online data-centric litigation cases. Digital ad markets are a technology and big data-driven sector where complexity increases the likelihood of fraudulent behavior.[7] Advertising fraud is an area where there have been few, if any, major cases like *Pulaski* till now. However, cases are beginning to slowly emerge like *Uber v. Fetch Media*. In this ongoing case, the ridesharing application Uber alleges its partner responsible for advertising campaigns, Fetch Media, defrauded Uber by purchasing nonexistent, nonviewable, and/or fraudulent online ads.[8] With increased awareness, major litigation in this complex, Big Data-driven sector is highly likely in the near future; however, such cases will be difficult. Analytical and legal approaches to such cases will, by necessity, be complex and novel.

One interesting subset of internet advertising fraud which may make its way into the courts is known as "Fake Influencer" fraud. Social media influencers (SMIs) are consumers, or ideally celebrities, with large numbers of followers on social media that marketers engage to promote their brands. Marketers use these influencers in a number of ways, including product placements, to increase brand engagement or awareness. For example, an influencer may make YouTube videos or Instagram posts advertising or highlighting a company's product. Such marketing can be quite lucrative for influencers, and quite costly for advertisers; one of the highest paid celebrities, Kim Kardashian, receives between $300,000 and $500,000 per sponsored Instagram post.[9]

Marketers and brands are rapidly expanding their spending on SMIs, as they deem it a highly effective approach to reach target consumer demographics. Brands increasingly seek out influencers to create content and build awareness about their products and services. Influencers are deemed valuable at any level, whether they have 200 social media followers or 1 million.[10] However, as brands rely on influencers to educate, build awareness, and drive sales among their target demographic, the system invites allegations of abuse and fraud. SMIs can inflate their followers or create bots pretending to be real humans, which allows these influencers to fraudulently bill advertisers, erode business ROIs, and damage consumer

[7] Roberto Cavazos, May 2019, *Global Ad Fraud May Cost up to $95 Billion Annually*. Special report Cheq.Ai and University of Baltimore.

[8] See https://www.courthousenews.com/wp-content/uploads/2017/09/Uber-v-Fetch.pdf

[9] See https://www.tubefilter.com/2019/05/10/kim-kardashian-500000-per-sponsored-post

[10] *What Every Marketer Needs to Know About Influencer Marketing and Buying Followers*. Marketing News, February 2019.

trust.[11] Fraud in this sector is estimated at between $750 and $1.5 billion per year.[12]

However, influencers can themselves be targeted and manipulated by fraudulent advertisers. In 2017 the creator of the Frye music app, Billy McFarland, devised a fraudulent music festival to take place in the Bahamas, Frye Festival, to promote his app. The scandal led to several prominent court cases: McFarland was sentenced to six years in prison, while other organizers were subjects of several civil fraud suits seeking as much as $100 million in damages for defrauding ticket holders.[13] Uniquely, the Frye Festival relied on social media influencers and celebrities to promote the festival, without the celebrities or SMIs realizing they were promoting a fraudulent music festival.[14]

The issue of trust and authenticity in influencer marketing is such that the US Federal Trade Commission (FTC) has now intervened, issuing guidelines to ensure consumers are not manipulated by fake influencers and fraudulently sponsored content.[15] Despite these new guidelines, one can expect that the continued growth of such Big Data enterprises will be followed by corresponding growth in litigation and case complexity. Courts, attorneys, experts, and the entire legal profession will have to improve their understanding of both online commerce and the data that goes along with it.

Finally, allegations and litigation over fraudulent advertising will likely increase in the coming years. Conceptually, ad fraud is driven by complex market structures. Calls for greater transparency by some industry participants will be found moot, as has been the case in other complex markets. Complex market structures transform extremely slowly, and, at present, instances of ad fraud are technologically enabled. Ultimately, fraudulent behavior in online advertising will be caused by information asymmetry generated by this increased complexity.

[11] Roberto Cavazos, *The Cost of Fake Influencers, Special Report*, Cheq.ai and University of Baltimore, July 2019.

[12] Megan Cerullo, "Influencer marketing fraud will cost brands $1.3 billion in 2019" CBS News, July 24, 2019.

[13] *Fyre: The Greatest Party That Never Happened*. Directed by Chris Smith. Los Gatos, CA: *Jerry Media*, 2019.

[14] Bluestone, Gabrielle (April 29, 2017). "A National Punchline." Vice.

[15] See https://www.lexology.com/library/detail.aspx?g=0a8df00c-3831-4cf1-a994-477bb182abdf

Final Thoughts

Big Data and complex statistical methods are increasing components of federal court cases. Data-heavy cases do, and could, run the gambit of fraud, private torts, antitrust, discrimination, civil rights, and many more classes of legal cases. As public and private sources store increasingly larger and complex sources of information, litigants can utilize a variety of these sources in court to support their suits. The case studies cited are hardly exhaustive of the many different uses of expert witness testimony or Big Data, but these cases represent notable intersections of data and legal standards.

Disentangling data sources and analyzing the data are important factors for litigants on both sides of a case. What these cases demonstrate is the importance of how data-based evidence is presented to a court. Judges, as gatekeepers of expert witness testimony, are obligated to pay attention to the data's rigor and relevance. Data evidence developed from dubious methods is likely to be discounted or ultimately excluded. But even if a litigant's evidence survives a *Daubert* challenge, the court is not obligated to weigh the data evenly in its rulings. More often than not, the data produced by one side is challenged quite ferociously by opposing experts or litigants, who may present their own findings.

The litigants which succeed are those who can tie the data more closely to the legal standards that courts rely on in basing their judgments. Data used to support or refute a class certification, for example, should relate to the tests a plaintiff class has to meet. Parties analyzing fraudulent behavior allegations, for example, should be able to use the data to point to a specific injury.

Big Data is a powerful tool, but the evidence it generates can fall short of proving a case that turns on minor legal questions. The functionality and utility of Big Data in court will only become more defined as technology and analytical fields change with it. Courts, too, will have to adapt and become more aware of how data is compiled, generated, and analyzed.

Accuracy and relevance are equally important in a Big Data analysis presented in court. Ultimately, each side has to return to big picture questions. What issue in the case could data be utilized for as evidence? Is the data understandable and straightforward enough for the court to understand? What are its weaknesses? Finally, given what the data show, how does this support or refute the contentions in the case?

References

Bluestone, Gabrielle. "A National Punchline". Vice. April 29, 2017.

Cavazos, Roberto, *Global Ad Fraud May Cost up to $95 Billion Annually*. Special report Cheq. Ai and University of Baltimore, May 2019a.

Cavazos, Roberto, *The Cost of Fake Influencers, Special Report*, Cheq.ai and University of Baltimore, July 2019b.

Cerullo, Megan, "Influencer marketing fraud will cost brands $1.3 billion in 2019" CBS News, July 24, 2019.

Courthouse News, *Uber V. Fetch* September 2017. Via: https://www.courthouse-news.com/wp-content/uploads/2017/09/Uber-v-Fetch.pdf

eMarketer, Digital Ad Spending 2019, March 2019.

Fyre: The Greatest Party That Never Happened. Directed by Chris Smith. Los Gatos, CA: Jerry Media, 2019.

Texas Dept. of Housing and Community Affairs v. Inclusive Communities Project, Inc., 576 U.S. 135 S. CT 507 (2015).

United States Department of Justice, Office of Public Affairs, December 2018, Justice Department Recovers Over $2.8 Billion from False Claims Act Cases in Fiscal Year 2018. Via: https://www.justice.gov/opa/pr/justice-department-recovers-over-28-billion-false-claims-act-cases-fiscal-year-2018

United States of Department of Health and Human Services, Centers for Medicaid and Medicare Services, National Expenditures 2017 Highlights. Via: https://www.cms.gov/research-statistics-data-and-systems/statistics-trends-and-reports/nationalhealthexpenddata/nationalhealthaccountshistorical.html

What Every Marketer Needs to Know About Influencer Marketing and Buying Followers. Marketing News, February 2019.

CHAPTER 4

The Courts as Gatekeeper of Big Data Evidence

Abstract From 1923 until 1993, the admissibility of scientific evidence in the federal court system was governed by the standard set forth in *Frye v. United States.* In applying this standard, courts examined whether the proffered evidence had "gained general acceptance" in the particular field. In 1993, the Supreme Court decided *Daubert v. Merrell Dow Pharmaceuticals, Inc.*, and the court announced a new standard of admissibility for scientific evidence. This chapter illustrates how the Daubert standard has been applied to data analyses in US courts and its implication for Big Data as related cases become more frequent in the courts. Significantly, technological changes that make Big Data possible threaten to change the basis of current statistical reasoning and the basis upon which courts make decisions.

Keywords Daubert • Frye • Admissibility • Internet of Things • Bayesian statistical analysis

From 1923 until 1993, the admissibility of scientific evidence in the federal court system was governed by the standard set forth in *Frye v. United States.* In applying this standard, courts examined whether the proffered evidence had "gained general acceptance" in the particular field. Over the 70 years that followed its introduction, the Frye test penetrated both federal and state courts, governing the admissibility of scientific evidence of

D. Steward, R. Cavazos, *Big Data Analytics in U.S. Courts*,
Palgrave Advances in the Economics of Innovation and Technology,
https://doi.org/10.1007/978-3-030-31780-5_4

many kinds. In many jurisdictions, Frye even survived the different test of admissibility adopted by the Federal Rules of Evidence and its parallel state counterparts.

This changed in 1993. In 1993, the Supreme Court decided *Daubert v. Merrell Dow Pharmaceuticals, Inc.*, in which the court announced a new standard of admissibility for scientific evidence. The court held that the Federal Rules of Evidence displaced Frye. Thus, it found the appropriate standard of admissibility in Rule 702: "'If scientific, technical, or other specialized knowledge will assist the trier of fact to understand the evidence or to determine a fact in issue,' an expert 'may testify thereto.'"

Since the seminal 1993 Daubert Supreme Court decision, federal and state courts across the United States have taken on a role as gatekeeper of scientific, statistical, and ultimately Big Data evidence. The Daubert decision requires federal courts to apply certain criteria to determine if scientific evidence is admissible or not. These criteria include determining the reliability and known error rate of the analysis and the degree of acceptability of the methodology within the scientific community. In some legal jurisdictions, courts have established stringent guidelines for the admissibility of Big Data statistical evidence that require thorough vetting of the scientific evidence prior to trial.

This chapter illustrates how the Daubert standard has been applied to data analyses in US courts and its implication for Big Data as related cases invariably become more frequent in the courts. In addition, and most significantly, technological changes which have made Big Data possible also threaten to change the basis of some current statistical reasoning and thus the basis upon which courts make decisions.

The Daubert Standard and Big Data

The Daubert standard, as noted, is based on a trilogy of cases, *Daubert vs. Merrell Dow Chemicals* in 1993 which noted that Rule 702 of the Federal Rules of Evidence did not incorporate the Frye general acceptance test for admissibility of expert scientific testimony, but that the rule incorporated flexibility as a standard. Within this flexibility, several factors of consideration must be met.[1] These factors for a scientific theory, approach, technique, or methodology include:

[1] *Daubert v. Merrell Dow Pharmaceuticals, Inc.*, 509 U.S. 579 (1993).

- Whether an approach or technique has attracted widespread acceptance within the applicable or relevant scientific community.
- Whether a theory, technique, or method can and has been tested.
- The existence of standards for use or operation of the theory, technique, or method.
- Whether it has been peer reviewed.
- Known error rates or other limits.

Big Data Statistical Model Specification

Since the advent of the use of statistics there has been a reliance on theory. Economists devised models on the nature of phenomenon and confirmed these with sample data. Statisticians and social scientists of various types used surveys to obtain samples to draw inferences via hypothesis testing of populations, that is, the broader world. The courts, economists, and others have worked hard to make this knowledge useful in dispensing justice. However, the models which the courts and many experts on legal aspects of statistics and economics have grown accustomed to face some difficulties when deployed in a Big Data case.

The traditional methods of hypothesis testing and model specification are described and are based on the following:

> Traditionally, data analysis techniques have been designed to extract insights from scarce, static, clean and poorly relational data sets, scientifically sampled and adhering to strict assumptions (such as independence, stationarity, and normality), and generated and analyzed with a specific question in mind. The challenge of analyzing Big Data is coping with abundance, exhaustively and variety, timeliness and dynamism, messiness and uncertainty, high rationality, and the fact that much of what is generated has no specific question in mind or is a by-product of another activity. Such a challenge was until recently too complex and difficult to implement, but has become possible due to high-powered computation and new analytical techniques.[2]

This is evocative of the fact that up until the 1980s students in statistics (and in some cases economics) would take at least one if not more courses in statistical sampling. This was the norm. The need to become well

[2] Rob Kitchen, Big Data, new epistemologies and paradigm shifts, Big Data and Society, April 14, 2014.

acquainted with sampling techniques was essential for economists, statisticians, and social scientists to properly do their work. The need for this knowledge was driven by the scarcity and expense of computational space and storage. The sensibility stemming from old constraints (using small samples to test hypotheses, specifying models with a few variables) still inform how data is used in courts today. The challenge now is bridging the chasm between model testing and empirical Big Data discovery.

The Admissibility of Novel Statistical Big Data Analyses

A feature of any science including statistics is the constant progress and advance in the field. Like many fields such as medicine, physics, and mathematics, there are competing schools of thought in statistics into what methods best provide understanding into the phenomenon of interest. The use of novel methods needs to be robustly grounded in statistical best practice. For example, even well-trod established methods such as representative samples have been considered "impermissible." The US Supreme Court's 2011 decision in *Wal Mart Stores v. Dukes* rejected the idea of using a small sample of claims selected for adjudication to extrapolate class-wide liability and damages. This was noted as a refusal to engage in "trial by formula."

Then in 2016, the Supreme Court in *Tysons Foods vs. Bouaphakeo* approved the admissibility of "representative" evidence to prove class-wide liability and clarified that "Wal-Mart does not stand for the broad proposition that a representative sample is an impermissible means of establishing class wide liability."[3] The point is that well-known standard techniques of inferential statistics can be put under scrutiny and questioned by courts. Thus, in cases of the use of novel techniques particular care and rigor must be used.

Big Data features not only large amounts of data, it also is data with complex structures. The complexity in the structure of the data imposes challenges on the type of analysis to be undertaken as well as assessing the reliability of the data. A unique practical challenge is that methods of determining reliability and proper deployment are evolving and changing rapidly.

Big Data is characterized by "the 3 V's"; these are volume, velocity, and variety. Volume refers to the amount of data collected from transactions, activities, and measurements. Velocity refers to collecting data with high

[3] *Tyson Foods, Inc. v. Bouaphakeo*, 577 U.S. 136 S. Ct. 1036 (2016).

frequency and its availability for use and/or analysis. Variety refers to the various formats in which data are collected, transactions, images, scans, videos, linking of disparate data sources, and/or data types. All of these key features of data have unique attributes and pose challenges in gaining insights on reliability, especially in a legal setting.

Big Data analysis consists of the process of converting often disparate data into actionable information. This actionable information is used to support decisions and guide policy in organizations both public and private. The range of decisions supported by Big Data analysis can range from optimal scheduling of delivery routes, credit and hiring decisions, inventory and product selection, insurance premiums, and so on.

Big Data analysis reliability under Daubert seemingly poses a challenge given that Big Data analysis is in many ways novel. For example, some of the data discovery and other more generally known statistical methods used in Big Data analysis depart from well-known statistics which are cited in standard undergraduate textbooks.

Many people, including judges and potential jurors, have heard of and may be familiar with statistical terms such as margin of error, sampling, and descriptive statistics, such as averages and medians. Few jurors or persons generally are familiar with Big Data terms and techniques that are in fact generally accepted among practitioners. Few people have likely encountered terms such as "Forest and Trees analysis," "random forests," "*k*-means neighbors," and discriminant analysis that are routinely used in Big Data analyses. However, technological advances in both computing power and relatively inexpensive storage space have made many Big Data techniques that were impossible to do in the past routine procedures today.

In a sense, in some cases accessing the entire universe of data relevant to a matter reduces the need for some generally accepted inferential statistics that are taught in universities. If you have the entire universe of data, hypotheses testing to determine if a sample conforms to a population and drawing inferences from a sample is not necessary. As such, approaches now long familiar to the courts are no longer necessary and may be of limited use in some cases. The statement below enthusing about the possibilities of Big Data in 2008 apply with more force as of this writing.

> There is now a better way. Petabytes allow us to say: 'Correlation is enough.' ... We can analyze the data without hypotheses about what it might show. We can throw the numbers into the biggest computing clusters the world has ever seen and let statistical algorithms find patterns where science

> cannot... Correlation supersedes causation, and science can advance even without coherent models, unified theories, or really any mechanistic explanation at all. There's no reason to cling to our old ways.[4]

Evolving Areas of Research: Bayesian Analysis and the Internet of Things

Analyses that are novel are often difficult to view through the court's standard gatekeeping lens. Analyses based on Bayesian-based analytical models and the nascent cases that involve the data generated by the growing number of internet-connected things, like internet-enabled surveillance cameras and appliances, are two examples of this issue.

For example, the use of a type of statistics known as "Bayesian methods" is widespread in many sectors yet it is not commonly understood by many legal professionals. The best way to understand Bayesian statistical and analytical reasoning is to compare it to the better-known, classical frequentist approach to analytical reasoning. In the classical approach to statistical reasoning, a researcher starts with the proposition that the opposite of the research question at interest is true. For example, a researcher initially assumes in a discrimination case that the employer-defendant did not discriminate against the class of employees. The initial research proposition under the classical approach is consistent with the legal concept of "innocent until proven guilty."

Based on this initial research proposition, the researcher will then calculate the probability that the data in the case would be observed naturally (by random chance) if in fact the initial proposition were true. So, in the above example, the researcher will calculate the probability that the data, such as salary data, would be generated if the employer was not discriminating against the class of employees at issue in the lawsuit. Accordingly, if it is calculated that there is only a small chance that the data would have been generated by a chance and presumably unbiased process, then it is concluded that it is unlikely that the initial proposition is in fact true. A probability of 5% or less is generally viewed as a small chance that chance generated the observed outcome. For example, if it is observed that there is a 0.5% chance that a given salary outcome for similarly situated female and male employees would have been generated by random chance, then

[4] Chris Anderson, The End of Theory: The Data Deluge Makes the Scientific Method Obsolete, Wired, June 23, 2008.

it may be potentially concluded that the initial proposition that the employer is not discriminating against female employees is not true.

The initial proposition using Bayesian methods is formulated in a different manner from that of the classical approach. The Bayesian approach does not necessarily start with the initial research proposition of "innocent until proven guilty." Many Bayesian initial propositions are formulated in the exact opposite way. A Bayesian initial proposition may be something to the effect of "What is the probability that a person accused of a crime is guilty?" Based on this initial proposition, a finding that says that there is a large probability that this initial proposition is true is consistent with the person's guilty. Because the question is completely opposite from the classical approach, this finding is completely opposite of the classical approach that essentially concludes that the person is guilty if there is a small probability calculated in the analysis.

In an employment discrimination case, the initial research proposition may be something like, "If the employer is discriminating against female employees, what is the probability that similarly situated male and female employees would have the salary outcomes that are observed in the data?" In this instance, the initial Bayesian question starts with the presumption of guilt and then calculates the probability that the outcome would be generated naturally by chance. So if the researcher finds that there is a large probability that the outcome would have been generated if the employer was discriminating, then it may possibly be concluded under the Bayesian approach that the employer is in fact discriminating against female employees.

The use of Bayesian methods to devise algorithms reliant on Big Data to make "decisions" or identify patterns does fall in familiar territory of devising assumptions and priors in accordance with some theory or other a priori knowledge. The interaction of Big Data and Bayesian methods is obviously one where much complexity lies both in operationalizing a Bayesian approach interacting with Big Data and in the issue of what the data measures and whether the data is relevant or merely collected from habit, tradition, or other outdated practices.

Most undergraduate and even professional school statistics courses are based on non-Bayesian classical frequentist methods reliant on a series of assumptions, some of which are subject to dispute. Much like the cases noted above in the world of inferential statistics, a sample is taken, a hypothesis is tested, and we arrive at some conclusion of the population of interest for the matter at hand based on a probability calculation (p-value).

In cases reliant on frequentist inferential statistics the size of sample, its representativeness, and appropriate testing are in the main straightforward with issues typically arising in sampling plan and levels of significance. Thus, the issues are of particular implementation and not of underlying science or approach.

There have been numerous cases of Bayesian models being sources of models and practices subject to litigation. With Big Data, Bayesian approaches support DNA testing, credit decisions, housing, and employment decisions. Despite the power and broad use of Bayesian methods in a range of scientific applications, there has been and remains resistance in the legal world to Bayesian methods. For example, the following are noted by opponents of Bayesian methods:

- That due to the complexity of cases and non-sequential nature of evidence presentation, any application of Bayes would be too cumbersome for a jury to use effectively and efficiently.
- Probabilistic reasoning as required to use Bayesian models is not compatible with the law and generally accepted legal thinking.
- Having jurors to consider, or formulate, an opinion of the defendant's guilt during a trial violates the juror's obligation to keep an open mind until all evidence is in.

Though some of the objections to Bayesian methods elaborated by the well-known legal scholar Lawrence Tribe have been effectively addressed, the resistance to these methods in the legal community remains.[5] In fact, Bayesian analysis has faced strong criticism for centuries. Indeed, the approach was practically taboo among professional statisticians for much of its history, even though non-statistician practitioners used it to solve real-world problems. For example, Bayesian methods were used to crack the Nazi enigma code in World War 2, identifying the causes of lung cancer and heart disease.[6] As such, despite the ubiquity of Bayesian methods in a range of key uses in society, care in examining, presenting, and reviewing these in litigation is essential—as is rebutting in both word and

[5] Norman Fenton, Martin Neil, and Daniel Berger, Bayes and the Law, Annual Review of Statistics and Its Application 2016 3:1, 51–77.

[6] Mcgrayne, Sharon Bertsch, The Theory That Would Not Die: How Bayes' Rule Cracked the Enigma Code, Hunted Down Russian Submarines, and Emerged Triumphant from Two Centuries of Controversy. 2011, Yale University Press.

action the critiques listed above. A large factor in the increase in the ubiquity of Bayesian methods is due to improved computational technology since the 1970s when critiques against the method were strongly made.

Further, despite remaining resistance from some, Bayesian methods are widely used in regulation and law enforcement. For example, Bayesian Improved Surname Geocoding (BISG) is used by regulatory agencies such as the Federal Consumer Financial Protection Bureau (CFPB) to evaluate lenders' compliance with fair lending laws. BISG combines geography and surname-based information into a single proxy probability for race and ethnicity.[7] This is an example of the type of context within which Bayesian approaches are most commonly used, which typically are cases of discrimination or other forms of bias, fraud, or cheating of some type or another, and possession of drugs, weapons, or other illegal or hazardous item or attribute. Findings in several housing and mortgage cases have also relied upon Bayesian methodologies.

The nascent cases that involve the data generated by the growing number of internet-connected things, like internet-enabled surveillance cameras and appliances, are other examples of an evolving area for cases that have used Big Data-based evidence. Big Data and Big Data analysis are increasingly the basis for organizing and acting upon multiple aspects of people's lives. Health and auto insurance as well as financial institutions' core business decisions are increasingly reliant on their large stores of data and Big Data analytics and algorithms. These are at times flawed and have potentially devastating effects on individuals and business. There have been several high-profile instances of Big Data analysis and testing the limits of privacy and data security.

Big Data particularly in the guise of "Internet of Things" was central in the Seventh Circuit Court case *Naperville Smart Meter Awareness v. City of Naperville*, 900 F.3d 521 (7th Cir. 2018). This, unlike many cases, is centered on collection of Big Data. The case is characterized as having received little attention though it is thought to have broad impact on how courts interpret the Fourth Amendment in the emerging era of Big Data.

In this case (Naperville) the court heard an appeal regarding the city of Naperville's "smart meter" program. Without obtaining the permission of city residents the city of Naperville had been replacing standard electricity meters with "smart meters." Each of the smart meters collected thousands

[7] See Consumer Financial Protection Bureau, Using publicly available information to proxy for unidentified race and ethnicity. September 2014.

of readings a month from each residence, instead of just single monthly meter readings. According to the plaintiffs, the thousands of monthly readings of the "smart meters" collected so much data at a level of detail such that they could tell what type of appliances were present in homes and when they were used. Due to the potential impact on resident's privacy, the Seventh Circuit found that Naperville's collection of smart meter data from residents' homes constituted a "search" under the Fourth Amendment. However, the Seventh Circuit found that lack of consent by residents to extensive data collection by the smart meters was key to rendering that collection was a search.

Though the smart meter data's collection was deemed a search under the Fourth Amendment, the court then asked whether the search was reasonable. In affirmatively answering that question, the court considered the search's actual purpose. The search was being performed by the city's utility to improve the energy grid, increase efficiency, and reduce costs. Notably a city utility is not a law enforcement agency. Because the city of Naperville conducted the search with no enforcement intent, the court found the search reasonable.

This is a very interesting case in that it illustrates the pervasiveness of Big Data and how many view such Big Data as intrusive. Relative to other types of Big Data being generated, stored, analyzed, and used, having your local utility know whether you use a blow dryer, frequently play video games, or rely on a microwave to prepare family meals is relatively innocuous.

A recent Supreme Court decision is also illustrative of the power, use, and pervasiveness of Big Data. In June 2018, the Supreme Court issued an opinion in *Carpenter v. United States.* The court decided that a warrant is required for police to access cell phone location information from a cellphone carrier. Specifically, the detailed geolocation information generated by a cellphone's communication with cell towers. At issue in this case was whether cell-site location information (CSLI) could be accessed by law enforcement without a warrant.

CSLI is generated constantly as a phone communicates with a cell tower. In many instances the CSLI data is generated when sending a text message, using an app, or turning on the phone. Through any of these actions the phone communicates with the nearest cell tower. CSLI can also be generated *automatically* such as when a phone receives a call or when a phone sends a network update. The higher the density of cell towers, the more accurate the location data. Cellphone companies keep years of records of CSLI for business purposes. In short, finding out the details of a phone's movements for years is within the capabilities of a phone carrier.

References

Anderson, Chris. The End of Theory: The Data Deluge Makes the Scientific Method Obsolete, Wired, June, 23 2008.

Daubert v. Merrell Dow Pharmaceuticals, Inc., 509 U.S. 579 (1993).

Fenton, Norman, Martin Neil, and Daniel Berger, Bayes and the Law, Annual Review of Statistics and Its Application 2016 3:1, 51–77.

Kitchen, Rob. Big Data, new epistemologies and paradigm shifts, Big Data and Society, April 14, 2014.

Mcgrayne, Sharon Bertsch, The Theory That Would Not Die: How Bayes' Rule Cracked the Enigma Code, Hunted Down Russian Submarines, and Emerged Triumphant from Two Centuries of Controversy. 2011, Yale University Press.

Tyson Foods, Inc. v. Bouaphakeo, 577 U.S. 136 S. Ct. 1036 (2016).

United States Government, Consumer Financial Protection Bureau, Using publicly available information to proxy for unidentified race and ethnicity. September 2014. Via: https://www.consumerfinance.gov/data-research/research-reports/using-publicly-available-information-to-proxy-for-unidentified-race-and-ethnicity/

CHAPTER 5

Indirect Use of Big Data Analytics in US Courts

Abstract Big Data and generally accepted statistical knowledge are at the center of many decisions and rulings in US courts. Even in circumstances where statistics and Big Data knowledge are generally accepted, fact finders still need to be aware of, and in some instances scrutinize, the underlying assumptions of this generally accepted knowledge. In addition, the use of Big Data has grown dramatically in the last decade and many organizations are reliant on third parties to meet their actual or perceived data needs. In these instances, a customer cannot test drive and check under the hood of a Big Data solution and is at the mercy of a software vendor's product. This chapter illustrates the major issues with the use of Big Data.

Keywords Credit history • Hiring • Wrongful death and injury • Equity

Big Data and generally accepted statistical knowledge obtained from analyses of that data are at the center of any number of seemingly routine court decisions and rulings in US courts. The underlying assumptions regarding generally accepted knowledge about Big Data need to be fully understood, if not questioned, by fact finders. For instance, life expectancy tables, which are based on the analysis of massive amounts of historical death records data, are routinely used in personal injury cases to calculate economic damages for individuals who are injured by an alleged wrongful

D. Steward, R. Cavazos, *Big Data Analytics in U.S. Courts*,
Palgrave Advances in the Economics of Innovation and Technology,
https://doi.org/10.1007/978-3-030-31780-5_5

event. It is standard procedure to use life and mortality tables in these cases to determine a reasonable length of damages based on how long the injured person could have been expected to live had the allegedly harmful incident not occurred.

Even in circumstances where statistics and Big Data knowledge are more or less generally accepted, fact finders still need to be aware of, and in some instances scrutinize, the underlying assumptions of this generally accepted knowledge. For instance, life and mortality tables are generally not designed to calculate the life expectancy of any one individual. Instead, these types of tables are generally designed to calculate the average mortality for a large group of individuals. These types of tables cannot account for factors such as the individual's medical history, family medical history, or changes in medical technology over time. Fact finders at a minimum need to understand the underlying assumptions of even generally accepted statistical concepts. As noted, Big Data includes a great many well-known and a few arcane methodologies as well as complex linking across multiple databases and other data sources.

In addition, the use of Big Data has grown dramatically in the last decade and many organizations are reliant on third parties to meet their actual or perceived data needs. The Big Data industry has grown and there exist multiple firms providing what are known as "white label" solutions. In effect, a large-scale provider of data science services allows others to put their "brand" on a suite of services. These services are provided at attractive prices and much of the labor is often outsourced to low-labor-cost nations. There can in such instances be risks associated with using such services. In particular, a firm purchasing or leasing third party Big Data analytics software/solutions is typically unable to assess the rigor, adequacy, or actual usefulness of algorithms. A customer cannot test drive and check under the hood of a Big Data solution and is at the mercy of a software vendor's product.

This chapter illustrates the major issues with the use of Big Data.

Using Credit Information for Hiring

Noteworthy is the 2015 law passed by the New York City Council prohibiting the use of a person's credit history for employment purposes. The law is summarized as follows:

> It is an unlawful discriminatory practice for an employer, labor organization, or employment agency to use an employee's or applicant's consumer credit history for employment purposes or to otherwise discriminate against an employee or applicant with respect to hiring, compensation, or the terms, conditions or privileges of employment based on the employee's or applicant's consumer credit history. Specifically the law defines "consumer credit history" as: "an individual's credit worthiness, credit standing, credit capacity, or payment history, as indicated by (a) a consumer credit report; 3 (b) credit score; or (c) information an employer obtains directly from the individual regarding (1) details about credit accounts, including the individual's number of credit accounts, late or missed payments, charged-off debts, items in collections, credit limit, prior credit report inquiries, or (2) bankruptcies, judgments or liens."[1]

The law does not apply to employers required by state or federal law to use individual consumer credit histories for employment purposes.[2]

The fact is that, indeed, credit information is Big Data. However, credit information has a number of issues that may be reason for pause in some instances, such as the unknown and proprietary algorithms which comprise the credit score, the manner in which the items in the report are compiled, and the fact that at times the scores are flawed. In addition, from a public policy standpoint there is the reality that individuals through no fault of their own may experience unemployment or other misfortunes which could adversely affect their credit. Being denied employment on the basis of poor credit could only exacerbate an individual's economic situation.

Moreover, the empirical basis for using credit history in areas such as in hiring and employment has been questioned. Research has questioned the relationship between credit scores and employee performance ratings or disciplinary issues at work, for example.[3] The researchers concluded that their data indicate there is no benefit from using credit history to predict employee performance or turnover.

[1] See Baer Lawrence, Johal Kira. New York City Limits the Use of Credit and Criminal History to make Employment Decisions, Employee Relations Law Journal 37 Vol. 41, No. 3, Winter 2015.

[2] Ibid.

[3] Koppes Bryan, L., & Palmer, J. K. (2012). Do Job Applicant Credit Histories Predict Performance Appraisal Ratings or Termination Decisions? *The Psychologist-Manager Journal, 15*(2), 106–127. doi: https://doi.org/10.1080/10887156.2012.676883

Research does suggest that there is an important distinction between an individual's credit history and performance versus credit issues and risks in sensitive positions of public trust or financial responsibility. In addition, well-known issues in hacks of credit reporting or identity theft demonstrate the vulnerabilities of credit-reporting agencies and in turn these place burdens and risks on ordinary individuals with respect to credit scores. For example, a 2013 Federal Trade Commission study found that 26% of consumers surveyed had inaccurate information in their credit reports and that these mistakes were material for 13% of consumers in that they had experienced credit denials, higher rates of interest, and other less favorable terms on credit.[4] An example of this is a well-documented report of an individual, a 69-year-old veteran, who lost his home due to erroneously reported debt for a credit card he never had.[5]

In a recent case, *Clark*, et al. *v. Experian Info. Sols. Inc.*, Case No. 3:16-cv-00032, and *Brown*, et al. *v. Experian Info. Sols. Inc.*, Case No. 3:16-cv-00670, both in the US District Court for the Eastern District of Virginia, Experian agreed to free credit monitoring in a settlement to resolve claims that the credit agency improperly reported public records which in turn adversely affected claimants. It was alleged that Experian failed to put appropriate processes to insure the veracity of public records such as tax liens and judgments. As is true of any Big Data organization, Experian collects, compiles, and analyzes data from many disparate sources. The class action claims and settlement in the Experian case demonstrate that there are risks in collecting and compiling information.

In response to these issues, there are currently multiple firms that are Big Data dependent that offer alternative credit scoring services drawn from algorithms which compile data from disparate data. From an economic viewpoint, it is clear that advances in Big Data-based credit-reporting approaches provide benefits and make obtaining credit easier. However, errors or other issues such as data breaches that divulge sensitive information are real social, personal, and ultimately litigation risks.

[4] See Federal Trade Commission Report to Congress, Under Section 319 of the Fair Trade and Accurate Credit Transactions Act of 2003 (December 2012).

[5] Hunter Stewart, Its disturbing your credit report is wrong, Huntington Post (August 11, 2014).

Using Big Data to Hire New Employees that Fit the Firm's Environment

Personality assessments have been used for a century to determine if a potential employee's various attributes are such as to function effectively in the organization or in a particular role. Though used widely and for some time it does not imply that these assessments have been without significant flaws. Currently virtually many personnel recruiters and human resources department have ready access to potential employee Big Data with sites like Glassdoor, LinkedIn, and Google+, which are full of employment-specific data (experience, education, skills, and location).

Using advanced search capabilities on these sites or commercial talent management systems can help human resource departments and recruiters get a clear sense of their candidate pools and use more sophisticated processes to recruit the talent they seek. As impressive as this is and indeed on many levels a technological breakthrough, there are many potential issues which can impact firms, individuals, and society at large. In particular, some of the features of selection algorithms are designed or have been indirectly "trained" in a fashion such that some subset of applicants may be excluded from candidate pools. In many instances, the algorithm is not necessarily designed to exclude but instead includes certain candidates by focusing on features and characteristics that may be more prevalent in one group than in another group.

Efficiency, Fairness, and Big Data

Economists and economic theory deals with issues of efficiency and generally areas related to fairness and equity to policy makers, researchers in other areas, and the public. However, in some litigation, neutral and unbiased analyses based on Big Data can in fact create situations that may be unpalatable to certain groups and subsets of the population. The calculation of economic damages in personal injury and wrongful death litigation is one such example.

In calculating economic damages for personal injury and wrongful death cases, economists use Big Data-based sources, such as mortality and work life tables. These types of tables provide the economist with projections of how long individuals can be expected to live and how long they can be expected to work. In personal injury and wrongful death litigation, economists use this information to determine how long the person would have lived and worked had they not been killed or injured by the alleged wrongdoing of the defendant. Generally, the longer a person is expected to live and work, the higher the economic damages would be.

The life and work life tables that economists utilize are based on millions of individual records and are generally accepted in the profession and widely used. The tables are also broken down by different demographic factors such as gender and race. As is not surprising, the tables, which are based on a massive amount of historical data, indicate that different groups of people have different life expectancies and work life expectancies. The accurate calculation of economic damages requires the incorporation of this information into the formulation of an individual's alleged economic loss.

However, as a result of the incorporation of this type of information, certain groups will receive smaller economic damage awards and settlements. A number of groups such as the National Association for the Advancement of Colored People (NAACP) Legal Defense Fund, Lawyers' Committee for Civil Rights Under Law, the Washington Lawyers' Committee, the National Employment Lawyers Association, and others have attempted to raise awareness of this issue to the legal community. There are at least two states, New Jersey and Arizona, that require the use of blended race and gender tables. In 2016, bills were introduced in the Senate and the House that sought to prohibit federal courts from awarding civil damages using calculations for the projected future earning potential that took into account the race, ethnicity, gender, religion, or actual or perceived sexual orientation of the plaintiff.

These types of Big Data issues will arise and not doubt have to be addressed as the use of these types of data continues.

References

Baer Lawrence, Johal Kira. New York City Limits the Use of Credit and Criminal History to make Employment Decisions, Employee Relations Law Journal 37 Vol. 41, No. 3, Winter 2015.

Hunter Stewart, Its disturbing your credit report is wrong, Huntington Post (August 11, 2014).

Koppes Bryan, L., & Palmer, J. K. (2012). Do Job Applicant Credit Histories Predict Performance Appraisal Ratings or Termination Decisions? *The Psychologist-Manager Journal*, *15*(2), 106–127.

United States Federal Trade Commission Report to Congress, Under Section 319 of the Fair Trade and Accurate Credit Transactions Act of 2003 (December 2012).

CHAPTER 6

Future Challenges and Recommendations

Abstract The courts, both state and federal, will need to evolve as the use of Big Data grows in the United States. In the coming years, courts will no doubt see more Big Data analyses with even more data being analyzed. The techniques of statistics, and the supporting computing power, are improving at such a rate such that we can now analyze entire populations so the need in some cases for inferences based on samples is lessened. The technology surrounding Big Data is starting to disrupt how evidence is considered and in fact what constitutes evidence in the court setting. Some areas that are going to be important as courts make that evolution are discussed in this chapter.

Keywords Artificial Intelligence • Smart Contracts • Constitutional rights • Privacy

Big Data and its associated technologies such as Machine Learning and Artificial Intelligence (AI) are considered by many observers as some of the most important advances in technology in the last century. These changes are having and will continue to have far-ranging impacts in the way we work, how we do business, how we govern, and ultimately how we live. It will also significantly impact how some cases are litigated in US courts.

D. Steward, R. Cavazos, *Big Data Analytics in U.S. Courts*,
Palgrave Advances in the Economics of Innovation and Technology,
https://doi.org/10.1007/978-3-030-31780-5_6

The courts, both state and federal, will need to evolve as the use of Big Data grows in the United States. In the coming years, courts will no doubt see more Big Data analyses with even more data being analyzed. The techniques of statistics, and the supporting computing power, are improving at such a rate such that we can now analyze entire populations so the need in some cases for inferences based on samples is lessened. The technology surrounding Big Data is starting to disrupt how evidence is considered and in fact what constitutes evidence in the court setting.

Below are some areas that are going to be important as courts make that evolution.

1. **Court Big Data Handbooks**. Courts at the federal and state level need to expand current handbooks on scientific evidence and discuss the more recent developments in data science, especially as they relate to Big Data. Courts need to be able to question the foundations of Big Data and statistical analyses based on its use. There is a need to codify and/or place in a compendium the key foundational aspects of classical and alternative statistical approaches such as Bayesian techniques and Big Data analytics. As noted above, some are of the considered opinion that due to the ubiquity of data and ability to use Big Data, there is a paradigm shift in how data analysis is conducted. Court handbooks should be augmented with the crucial distinction between cases where inferential statistics and sampling techniques are necessary and those cases where the amount and characteristics of data constitute a data universe and thus descriptive and correlation analyses are appropriate.
2. **Novel Evidence.** Courts will need to be able to deal with new and novel statistical methods. For example, much of what is seen in courts is based on traditional frequency-based statistics but social sciences are routinely relying on other types of data such as Bayesian and nonparametric statistics. Recommendation: Outside panel of experts evaluating the standing of the methodology in the profession (but not the merits) of each side's statistical argument.
3. **Artificial Intelligence**. As much as administrative and behavioral data captured through various means has and will continue to affect society and litigation, the current and potential impact of Artificial Intelligence (AI) will be immense. What is AI? The first use of the term is commonly agreed to have emerged from a 1955 paper by John McCarthy, Marvin L. Minsky, Nathaniel Rochester, and

Claude E. Shannon, *A Proposal for the Dartmouth Summer Research Project on Artificial Intelligence*. The authors noted: *An attempt will be made to find how to make machines use language, form abstractions and concepts, solve kinds of problems now reserved for humans, and improve themselves ... For the present purpose the artificial intelligence problem is taken to be that of making a machine behave in ways that would be called intelligent if a human were so behaving.* AI refers to the use of statistical algorithms which are trained to observe patterns in data. The data can be numerical in either counts or measures, visual, audio, or complex scenarios. From this data, computers deploying algorithms can "learn" tasks. Such use may be personal, medical, military, commercial, or industrial.

The issue of legal liability will become pressing when an autonomous driving vehicle is involved in an accident, when the factory robot injures a worker, when the trading algorithm is part of financial fraud, and when an employment algorithm discriminates. Who is legally liable? Company leadership? The programmer? The mathematician who devised the algorithm? The implementer of the algorithm? The software? Who?

4. **AI and the Practice of Law**. Aside from the nature of cases, AI may potentially change the very nature of how law is practiced. In the fall of 2018, Harvard Law School's Library Innovation Lab had successfully managed to scan and digitize more than 40 million legal documents related to every reported US state and federal case from the 1600s to summer 2018. This accomplishment is remarkable and very significant on many levels. Beyond the interests of archivists and preservationists, this project, known as the Caselaw Access Project, which is free and accessible to everyone, is seen as ideal for the several developers who are working on legal AI systems. According to a legal tech journalist in June of 2018:

> Harvard Law School's Caselaw Access Project, which last year completed a massive project to digitize all U.S. case law, this week released a tool called Historical Trends that allows a user to visually graph the frequency of words and phrases in those cases over time. The tool is similar in function to the Google Books Ngram Viewer, which allows users to graph the frequency with which phrases have appeared in a corpus of books over time. The Historical Trends tool can be used to search for phrases of up to three words and to compare multiple phrases. It also allows wildcard

searching. Users can limit searches to specific jurisdictions. Results can be shown as a graph over time or in a table view. Once you enter a query and generate a graph, you can click anywhere on the graph to create a list of "example cases" that show the use of the phrase within that time span. From the example cases, you can then conduct a search for the phrase in the full collection.[1]

5. **Algorithms and Machine Learning**. What are Algorithms (AI) and Machine Learning (ML)? Companies are already using AI to assess their employees. And commentators are already expressing concern that AI may thereby reinforce biases and may do so in ways that make legal redress difficult. Our current legal doctrines do not necessarily lend themselves to policing companies that rely on AI, even when the AI relies on analyses that might well be impermissible if undertaken by human beings. Is there ever discriminatory intent, for example, when it comes to data mining and artificial reasoning? And are such efforts—by design—necessarily job related and consistent with business necessity. The statistician and author Kathy O'Neal in her book *Weapons of Math Destruction* notes several cases where improperly designed algorithms have enormous adverse impacts on peoples' lives. Algorithms may in the main be beneficial but have in many instances due to flaws and/or biases of their creators wrongfully led to denial of credit and employment. In other cases, algorithms have adversely affected businesses. More dramatically, in several cases algorithms have led to imprisonment, loss of child custody, and even death.[2]
6. **Smart Contracts.** A "Smart Contract" can be defined as a legal agreement that contains or exists in the form of an algorithm. Unlike a traditional contract, which only lays out the terms of agreement for subsequent execution, a Smart Contract autonomously executes some or all of the terms of the agreement. A Smart Contract can be extraordinarily sophisticated and complicated, executing via the internet, for example, transactions at different costs and dates depending upon data such as currency exchange rates, stock market prices, costs of given raw materials, and anticipated weather

[1] See Ambrogi Bob. New Historical Trends Viewer from Caselaw Access Project Graphs Frequency of Words and Phrases, Law Sites, June 21, 2018.

[2] O'Neil, Cathy. *Weapons of Math Destruction: How Big Data Increases Inequality and Threatens Democracy*. Unabridged. New York: Random House, 2016.

conditions. Notwithstanding their names, Smart Contracts are actually fairly "dumb" as they ultimately rely on code that contains a set of instructions determining what happens when certain circumstances occur. In this sense, even though they self-execute—thus not requiring any human intervention or any other form of intelligence—they remain "computable contracts" which rely on being provided with data relevant to compliance or performance. From a programming point of view, Smart Contracts are generally based on blockchains, a technology that permanently records transactions in a way that cannot be later erased but can only be sequentially updated, in essence keeping a never-ending historical trail. Originally created to support crypto-currencies such as Bitcoin, the distributed ledger technology behind blockchains is now being used in other fields.

7. **Constitutional Rights, Privacy, and Big Data**. There are multiple issues associated with matters of Constitutional Rights, privacy, and Big Data. One issue is whether or not data is considered free speech. There are also issues of appropriate use of personal data (financial, health, educational, legal) and safeguards of data to name a few. Privacy and free speech were much linked in earlier times but we are now in a world of information, both private and public, which drives the economy. Information (data) is key in the information age; as noted above, information influences how everything functions. *Throughout the world, democratic societies regulate personal data using laws that embody Fair Information Practices (FIPs). The FIPs are one of the most important concepts in privacy law. They are a set of principles that regulate the relationships between business and government entities that collect, use, and disclose personal information about "data subjects"—the ordinary people whose data is being collected and used. Perhaps ironically, the FIPs were developed by the United States government in the 1970s because the government wanted to establish some minimal best practices for the processing of personal data.*[3]

From this work emerged "basic principles" to which data systems must adhere. These are: (1) There must be no personal data record-keeping systems whose existence is secret. (2) There must be a way for an individual to find out what information about him is in

[3] See, Richards, Neil "Why Data Privacy Law is Mostly Constitutional," William and Mary Law Review, Volume 56, Issue 4, Article 12.

a record and how it is used. (3) There must be a way for an individual to prevent information about him that was obtained for one purpose from being used or made available for other purposes without his consent. (4) There must be a way for an individual to correct or amend a record of identifiable information about him.

An organization creating, maintaining, using, or disseminating records of identifiable personal data must assure the reliability of the data for their intended use and must take precautions to prevent misuse of the data. A review of the five basic principles shows that as information and its use have become much more ubiquitous since their promulgation in the 1970s, the risk of any if not all of these principles being violated has increased astronomically. Data breaches of government databases, identity theft, hacking, improper use of data, doxing of individuals using "private" data are all frequent occurrences. In 2017 Equifax, a major credit-reporting firm, reported a data breach in which 143 million Americans were and remain exposed to a lifetime of identity theft.[4] In 2018, phone company T-Mobile was hacked and 2 million accounts had passwords, payment methods, and other information compromised.[5]

8. **Big Data Risks.** In September of 2018, the American Civil Liberties Union (ACLU) filed with the Equal Employment Opportunity Commission (EEOC) a charge of discrimination against Facebook. The charge had to do with Facebook's employment advertising practices.[6] More recently, Michigan Attorney Dana Nessel issued letters to three companies demanding information about a data breach affecting 12 million people around the country. The breach involved three large medical sector firms, American Medical Collection Agency (AMCA), Quest Diagnostics, and Optum360.[7] It is noted in the press release: "New York-based AMCA provides medical debt collection services to Quest Diagnostics and other health providers and health plans that have not yet been named. Optum360 contracted with AMCA to provide services to Quest. The breach affected 12 mil-

[4] Snider, Mike. Your data was probably stolen in cyberattack in 2018-and you should probably care. USA TODAY Dec. 28, 2018.

[5] Leskin, Page, The 21 Scariest Data Breaches of 2018, Business Insider. Dec. 30, 2018.

[6] Sheridan Robert, Cohen, Bret A, Big Data Analytics May Haunt Employers, New York Law Journal, November 2, 2018.

[7] See June 9, 2019, Press Release https://www.michigan.gov/ag

lion of Quest's patients, whose personal information was maintained by AMCA. It does not appear that AMCA has provided any public notice of this breach." What becomes clear here is that this is not a breach or loss of a large data set; this incident is illustrative of (1) the prevalence of Big Data (disparate data sources and parties exchanging and sharing data) and (2) the risks that Big Data poses to a particular party as a result of the actions or errors of a third party.

More troubling and exposed in the Michigan AG action is that there appear to be limited means to compel firms experiencing a data breach to inform government of data breaches. Consider further statements from Michigan Attorney General Dana Nessel: "This data breach is yet another example of how fragile our information infrastructure is, and how vulnerable all of us are to cyber hacking," said Attorney General Dana Nessel. "And here in Michigan, we continue to rely on media reports that alert us to these terrible situations because – unlike most other states – we have no law on the books that requires that our office be notified when a breach occurs. I am determined to get information quickly and accurately to take steps to protect our residents." "Quest is only one of AMCA's medical clients, so it is possible that patient information from other healthcare providers may have also been breached. We have no idea how far and wide this breach has gone."

Further: "Nessel's office determined that Quest reported to the US Securities and Exchange Commission that, between August 1, 2018, and March 30, 2019, an unauthorized user had access to AMCA's system, which included financial information (credit card numbers, bank account information) medical information and other personal information (including social security numbers)."[8]

Another very significant breach of data in 2017 was that of credit-reporting agency Equifax. In many ways, credit-reporting organizations were among the first major users of Big Data. Though the precise algorithms used for generating credit scores are unknown, what is known is that data from multiple sources is shared with these organizations and these data are in turn used to generate credit scores. As a result of the 2017 data breach, in July 2018 Equifax agreed to pay $575 million and possibly up to $700 million as part

[8] Ibid.

of a global settlement with the Federal Trade Commission (FTC), the Consumer Financial Protection Bureau (CFPB), and 50 US states and territories, which alleged that the credit-reporting company's failure to take reasonable steps to secure its network led to a data breach in 2017 that affected approximately 147 million people.[9] The incident was of such a magnitude that the Commission vote authorizing the staff to file the complaint and proposed stipulated final order was 5-0. The FTC filed the complaint and proposed order on July 2019 in the US District Court for the Northern District of Georgia.

In a classic case of Big Data failure the FTC in its complaint alleged that Equifax "failed to secure the massive amount of personal information stored on its network, leading to a breach that exposed millions of names and dates of birth, Social Security numbers, physical addresses, and other personal information that could lead to identity theft and fraud." Further, in its press release the FTC provides detail on the settlement matter: "As part of the proposed settlement, Equifax will pay $300 million to a fund that will provide affected consumers with credit monitoring services. The fund will also compensate consumers who bought credit or identity monitoring services from Equifax and paid other out-of-pocket expenses as a result of the 2017 data breach. Equifax will add up to $125 million to the fund if the initial payment is not enough to compensate consumers for their losses. In addition, beginning in January 2020, Equifax will provide all US consumers with six free credit reports each year for seven years—in addition to the one free annual credit report that Equifax and the two other nationwide credit-reporting agencies currently provide."[10] Equifax also agreed to pay $175 million to 48 states, the District of Columbia and Puerto Rico, as well as $100 million to the CFPB in civil penalties.

[9] See Equifax to Pay $575 Million as Part of Settlement with FTC, CFPB, and States Related to 2017 Data Breach. Settlement includes fund to help consumers recover from data breach. Press release, July 22, 2019. U.S. Federal Trade Commission. Accessed July 22, 2019, https://www.ftc.gov/news-events/press-releases/2019/07/equifax-pay-575-million-part-settlement-ftc-cfpb-states-related

[10] Ibid.

Concluding Thoughts

As previously noted, hypothesis testing is well understood in the courts and by the lay public. Frequentist and sampling approaches are not going away any time soon and will be deployed in a range of litigation types. The Big Data revolution may change the understanding and use over time if current advances proceed at the current rate. The increase in the number and frequency of cases in which Big Data plays a key role will only increase. As noted above, and with even casual observation of developments and changes in the world, Big Data will continue to drive the functioning of an increasing number of key institutions in the world and in the United States.

Government at all levels, healthcare, business large and small are increasingly reliant on Big Data and its analysis to support and improve their operations. The supporting factors such as algorithms, Artificial Intelligence, Machine Learning, and other techniques and innovations will also come to impact more and more decisions and ultimately people. A once provocative but no longer unusual perspective expressed by many data scientists working at the cutting edge of Big Data was expressed in 2009: "scientists no longer have to make educated guesses, construct hypotheses and models, and test them with data-based experiments and examples. Instead, they can mine the complete set of data for patterns that reveal effects, producing scientific conclusions without further experimentation."[11]

The foregoing is highly relevant in the world of complex litigation. In effect, why worry about samples and hypothesis if you have the entire relevant universe of data available? Still, there will remain questions as to the integrity of the data, its validity and reliability, and crucially what if any algorithms and measurement assumptions were made. Though on the surface it would appear that having the entire universe of data is an unalloyed good, the reality is that the world of Big Data will bring a great deal of uncertainty and complexity to the world of complex litigation. In the next few years, those engaged in the world of complex litigation will have to learn new paradigms, rely on new knowledge and expertise, in their various roles. Awareness raising, new training for legal professionals, and continuing to highlight the work of scholars and practitioners who are at the vanguard of Big Data and the law is essential.

[11] Prensky M (2009) H. sapiens digital: From digital immigrants and digital natives to digital wisdom. *Innovate* 5(3).

We are at present in a transitional period where after many years and landmark cases approaches to weighing statistical evidence painstakingly developed by jurists, lawyers, regulators and expert witnesses will have to coexist with the realities of fundamental changes in approaching the discovery of knowledge. As is true in the case of any fundamental and important social, technological, and scientific change, the transitional period where two approaches of understanding the world coexist will pose many challenges. Ultimately, it is our hope that increasing understanding of Big Data among legal professionals will only provide new insights that will assist litigants and courts better adjudicate their cases.

References

Equifax to Pay $575 Million as Part of Settlement with FTC, CFPB, and States Related to 2017 Data Breach Settlement includes fund to help consumers recover from data breach. Press release, July 22, 2019. U.S. Federal Trade Commission. Accessed July 22, 2019. Via: https://www.ftc.gov/news-events/press-releases/2019/07/equifax-pay-575-million-part-settlement-ftc-cfpb-states-related

Leskin, Page. Dec. 30, 2018, The 21 Scariest Data Breaches of 2018, Business Insider.

Prensky M. H. Sapiens digital: From digital immigrants and digital natives to digital wisdom. *Innovate* 5(3) (2009).

Richards, Neil M. "Why Data Privacy Law is Mostly Constitutional", William and Mary Law Review, Volume 56, Issue 4, Article 12.

Sheridan, Robert O., Bret A. Cohen, Big Data Analytics May Haunt Employers, New York Law Journal, November 2, 2018.

Snider, Mike. Your data was probably stolen in cyberattack in 2018-and you should probably care. USA TODAY Published 6:00 a.m. ET Dec. 28, 2018.

Index[1]

[1] Note: Page numbers followed by 'n' refer to notes.

D. Steward, R. Cavazos, *Big Data Analytics in U.S. Courts*,
Palgrave Advances in the Economics of Innovation and Technology,
https://doi.org/10.1007/978-3-030-31780-5

The manufacturer's authorised representative in the EU is Springer Nature Customer Service Centre GmbH, Europaplatz 3, 69115 Heidelberg, Germany. If you have any concerns regarding our products, please contact ProductSafety@springernature.com

Printed and bound by CPI Group (UK) Ltd, Croydon, CR0 4YY
25/09/2026
02222890-0009